Tony Monette

I AM
JUSTIFIED

BEYOND THE HORIZON

BEYOND THE HORIZON

Five Years with the Khmer Rouge

LAURENCE PICQ

Translated by PATRICIA NORLAND

ST. MARTIN'S PRESS • NEW YORK

Library of Congress Cataloging-in-Publication Data

Picq, Laurence.
   Beyond the horizon.
   "A Thomas Dunne book."
   1. Cambodia—History—1975–   . 2. Pol
Pot.   3. Cambodia—Description and travel—1975–
4. Picq, Laurence—Journeys—Cambodia. I. Title.
DS554.8.P53 1989   959.6'04 [B]   88-36240
ISBN 0-312-02871-7

First Edition

10 9 8 7 6 5 4 3 2 1

A Thomas Dunne Book

First published in France by Éditions Bernard Barrault

· *Foreword* ·

Cambodia, or Kampuchea. Nation in Southeast Asia, 69,898 square miles (181,035 square kilometers). About 7,700,000 inhabitants in 1975 (more than one million were massacred between 1975 and 1979). Capital: Phnom Penh.

A former French protectorate (since 1863), Cambodia gained its independence in 1946 but remained associated with France. It did not gain complete political independence until 1954 (with the Geneva Conference), finally leaving the French Union in 1955.

On March 18, 1970, General Lon Nol took power in a coup d'état and proclaimed the Khmer Republic on October 9; but the former leader, Norodom Sihanouk, in exile in Peking, formed another government there, the Cambodian Royal Government of National Union (GRUNK). After five years of resistance against American intervention, the Khmer Rouge, having formed the National United Front of Kampuchea (FUNK) with Sihanouk, succeeded in its offensive to liberate Phnom Penh on April 17, 1975; Sihanouk returned to Phnom Penh in September 1975 but then resigned following the creation of Democratic Kampuchea (April 1976). Pol Pot then came to power. The Khmer Rouge attempted to establish a rural communism, forcing urban populations to evacuate to the countryside, destroying all economic activity, and abolishing the banking system. Vietnam invaded Cambodia in January 1979.—From *Le Petit Robert*, tome 2 (1982).

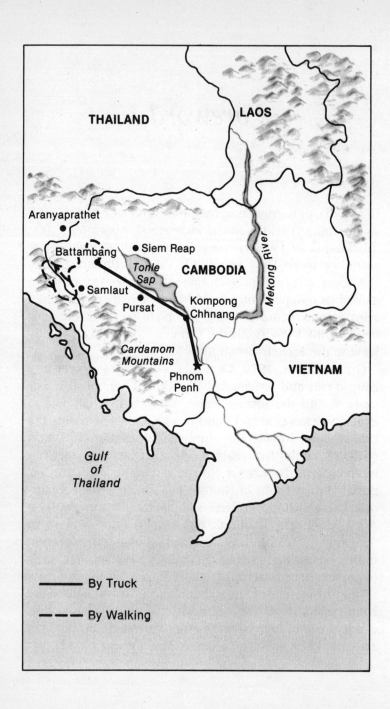

· *One* ·

It was cold that morning at the Peking airport. Winter had just returned, and the Chinese had once again donned their heavy padded clothing.

It was October 10, 1975. I was about to depart and was having trouble leaving this city in which I had lived for six years, Peking the Gentle, Peking the Rough, with its severe winters, torrid summers, fleeting springs, and too-short autumns.

We were alone on the runway: seventy Cambodians, along with my daughters and me, all dressed in the black cotton uniform of the resistance and surrounded by Chinese friends who had come to salute our departure. For the "distinguished guests" that we were, China had chartered a special aircraft.

"*Zai Jian*, good-bye!"

"Thank you for your generous help."

"It was our duty."

"Always bring back the biggest successes possible in building socialism."

"Good-bye, *Zai Jian*!"

We were leaving for Cambodia, the first to return to Phnom Penh, which had been liberated six months before, on April 17. The faces of my companions all shared the same expression of pride and determination.

In my backpack, issued by the resistance and necessarily light, were a mosquito net, a small blanket, a dress and a spare shirt, toothpaste, soap, a pen, some paper, photos, and acupuncture needles. Recently, *Angkar*, the "Organization" (the omnipresent, faceless, ruling force), had demanded that all jewelry and valuables be turned in. I gave everything I possessed: a gold chain that my grandmother had been given by her mother, a string of pearls, a rose quartz necklace and another of amber, my engagement ring, my wedding band, and some pendants. At the risk of breaking the rules, I had kept only two watches, one my twenty-first birthday present, and the other, which I wore on my wrist, the last memento of my father.

I looked back and caught a glimpse of Leang Sirivouth, one of my husband's cousins, who stood timidly behind everybody. I beckoned and he approached. I gave him the last of my money.

"See you soon," I told him. "We will meet again in Phnom Penh."

Scarcely able to hide his emotion, he reiterated how much he regretted not being able to join us. As a secretary at the embassy, he had been asked to stay in Peking. He leaned down to embrace my two daughters. Three and four years old, dressed in black, hair cut short, gaily carrying their little backpacks, they had the look of budding partisans.

"We are going to find Daddy. Will you come see us soon?" they asked.

As I walked toward the platform, I was invited by a Chinese interpreter I knew well to approach an official who was standing apart from the crowd. He was the assistant chief of protocol.

"In the name of Prime Minister Chou En-lai, I wish you much success," he said to me.

Surprised and moved by this attention, esteemed as it

was unexpected, I mustered a few words in response: "You have taught me everything. Thank you for your warm hospitality. Thank you. May the well-loved Chinese prime minister recover his health quickly. Long life to President Mao! I hope that you and your comrades achieve greater and greater success. . . ."

Throughout my speech, the official continued to shake my hand. When I finished, he exclaimed: "But you speak Chinese very well!"

While touched, I was also unnerved. The decision I had made was loaded with consequences. I was suddenly afraid of the dangers that awaited me. For a moment, I hesitated. Maybe it was not too late to turn back. In Peking, I had made a place for myself. I was going to abandon everything for a hard life among people whose narrow-mindedness had already made me suffer. But I caught myself and smiled: "Thank you again. Good-bye."

In Phnom Penh, I was to rejoin my husband Sikoeun (sick·oohn). We had met seven years earlier in France, where he was a student and I a teacher. He had talked enthusiastically about his country and his people, explaining that very prominent Cambodian intellectuals had entered the resistance to establish a new society where justice and equality reigned. The liberated zones were spreading day by day, and the peasants were taking their destiny into their own hands and achieving a better life, sheltered from all oppression and exploitation. Sikoeun loved his country and his people. He introduced me to his friends, all of whom were confident about the future of their country and were completely devoted to it.

Immediately after the March 1970 coup d'état deposed Prince Sihanouk, Sikoeun decided to leave for Peking in order to judge the situation from a closer vantage point. He planned to join the resistance, which was undertaking a new battle. On July 7 of that year, I left France for the summer and went to join my husband in Peking.

Since early childhood, China had fascinated me. I was attracted to this fabulous world: Peking, the Imperial Palace, the Forbidden City, the Great Wall . . . I was intrigued with the poetry, the philosophy, Chinese symbolism . . .

I was very happy.

A few days after arriving, I was invited to a reception in honor of Sihanouk's return from Korea. Oblivious to protocol for national leaders—and especially to the welcoming of a prince—I had, in typical French fashion, taken liberties with timing. I arrived at the station late, to the horror of the entire Khmer community, and then remained stubbornly rooted on the platform, fascinated by the ballet of official cars and the crowd's movements. Suddenly a man with thick eyebrows appeared in front of me: Chou En-lai! "Welcome, welcome!" he said in French, extending his hand. I was overwhelmed.

At the end of summer, I gave up my plans to return to France and the studies and job that no longer held meaning for me. I intended to stay with my husband, to share his efforts and enthusiasm and, at the same time, to get to know China better, for that was where we were temporarily confined to living.

Bit by bit, however, my enthusiasm abated. Life in the Khmer community proved difficult. Patriotic exaltation led my exiled companions to exclude me from their concerns and activities. This feeling intensified when Ieng Sary, special envoy of the resistance, landed in Peking. I was expecting my first child. Ieng Sary insisted that I be excluded from all Cambodian community activities.

"The business of Cambodians is only for Cambodians," he stated forcefully. Thereafter, I was considered the intruder, the spy, the bad spirit. I tried in vain to protest and defend myself. I stressed my good will, but to no avail. In the end I let go and vented my spite: "What narrowness of spirit!" I declared.

Ieng Sary took it badly and remained resentful toward

me. He forbade me to renew my passport and then prevented me from declaring the birth of my daughter to the French civil authorities.

Faced with such hostility, I withdrew into myself and was isolated for a long time, cut off from my country of birth and excluded from my husband's community. Meanwhile, I kept studying Chinese, which allowed me to establish some comforting contact with the Chinese people nearby.

The birth of my second daughter did nothing to bring me closer to the Khmer community or my husband. To him, my existence was a handicap vis-à-vis his compatriots. Only after he was accepted and allowed to join the resistance did his—and the Cambodians'—attitude toward me completely change. I expressed joy in hearing he was going to join his comrades in battle, and people seemed pleased with this response. They praised my courage. Suddenly I found myself as included as I had been excluded. So the atmosphere during my last year in China was much improved. I took two long trips, one west to Yenan, the other south to Canton, and returned with extraordinary memories of these places. Everywhere I went, I found a relaxed atmosphere and a tremendous eagerness to work. I felt I was present at the awakening of a people, simple folk who radiated a striking dignity. It seemed to me a marriage of humankind and nature—the dawn of a new world. I cared passionately about the China that was emerging from its cultural revolution with new energies.

I forgot my disappointments and faced the future calmly.

Strangely, the news of Phnom Penh's liberation on April 17, 1975, generated little enthusiasm among the Khmers living in exile in Peking. Some made ready to return to Cambodia, while others prepared to continue their exile under other skies. I was gripped by indecision. I would have liked to continue my stay in China, where I still had so much to learn. Furthermore, I secretly preferred my Chinese friends to those made with such difficulty among my husband's compatriots.

As it happened, the Khmer community was forced to remain for months in Peking. The Organization delayed all departures.

I had often asked myself what it was that Angkar, this powerful and respected entity, was hiding. Literally, the Khmer term translates as "organization," but just what this organization included, no one really knew. Some said it symbolized the Communist party, or the Socialist party (which apparently had a minimal impact). Others said it comprised a group of collegial leaders. Still others stated that it represented an eminent personality.

The summer of 1975 was marked by my mother's visit and the return of my husband. I saw Sikoeun again on August 15, during an official reception organized in honor of the visiting Cambodian head of state, Khieu Samphan. Sikoeun had changed drastically. The man who tended toward stoutness had become emaciated. He no longer wore glasses, which accented the thinness of his face, his cheeks sunken and his eyes set deep in their sockets. He looked like an escapee from a concentration camp. What kind of suffering had he endured while I lived happily in Peking? I felt bad just thinking about it, and guilty for not having been at his side.

When we met, he talked about the revolution underway in Cambodia. He described the new life. People lived happily off the fruits of their labor. There were no longer exploiters or exploited. Money had been abolished. Criminality had disappeared along with prostitution and all of

6

the other ills of society. Neither famine nor unemployment existed.

Hearing him talk, I discovered a new man. He was calm, almost radiant, if one overlooked his terrible thinness. Freed of anxiety, he seemed to have found "enlightenment," as expressed in the revolutionary jargon of the time.

"In Cambodia, we are pursuing and deepening the Chinese experience," he told me. "We need you."

They *needed* me? I could be of use for something? Sikoeun had just struck a sensitive chord. I immediately forgot the past. All of my bad memories vanished.

Sikoeun guaranteed that if I joined him in Cambodia, the Organization would make sure that my daughters and I had good living conditions. Feeling that I was on the verge of a great adventure, a wonderful experience, perhaps without precedent, I decided to join him. The future shone radiantly ahead of us, as it had on the first day we met. Together we would contribute to the development of humanity.

At least, that is what I thought the morning I boarded the plane for Phnom Penh.

After four hours in the air, the stewardess announced that we were flying over Cambodia. The enthusiastic passengers let loose with thunderous applause. The plane skirted the Mekong River; it was the end of the rainy season, and as far as we could see, the countryside was flooded. Passengers pressed their faces against the windows, dashing in unison from one side of the plane to the other to discover here a water barrier, there a network of dams. The amused pilot accompanied their movements by banking on one wing and then the other. Each person tried to outdo the next in his or her enthusiasm and in expressing his or her patriotic desire to participate as soon as possible in the construction of a dam or the digging of a canal.

When we reached Phnom Penh, the plane circled twice over the city before landing. I admired the golden roof of the Royal Palace shimmering in the sun. I was surprised by how small the city was. It certainly was not Paris, nor was it Peking, but it sparkled like a jewel in its green jewelry box. I imagined the people there living contently as if part of one big family.

Moreover, I forgot Peking and Paris. My future was there, under my eyes, at my feet. I rejoiced at the thought of finding my husband. With our two little girls, we were going to start a life that would be happy and full, useful and generous.

When the plane landed and the roar of its engines died out, a strange feeling gripped me. I pushed forward with the others toward the exit. Suddenly we were all silent. No one was on the runway. I looked in vain for my husband. There was not a soul, not a single movement on the deserted concrete where burned and gutted planes lay stranded, the last souvenirs of battle. The war was still there, it seemed, frozen like the last photos sent out by foreign correspondents before the fall of the city. In the terminal, the hall was also deserted. We held our breath, no one dared move. I felt as if I had landed on a lifeless planet. Anxious and full of doubt, I glanced at the Chinese crew. They smiled, which comforted me.

Suddenly, as if from out of nowhere, a man approached us. I recognized him: it was Sirin, one of my husband's comrades. Without a word of welcome, he ordered us to get into the bus waiting outside, adding that it was forbidden to talk during the trip. This proved to be unenforceable, however, and private exchanges were carried on. We moved slowly in the direction he pointed. An old, battered van covered with graffiti—a survivor from former days—was parked at the entrance to the terminal.

We settled ourselves in the van, which then rumbled away from the terminal. My daughters clamored for their father, and I told them he no doubt had been held up by his work. But inside I felt increasingly anxious and lonely.

What was happening? Why did Sirin refuse to talk to me? Had it become counterrevolutionary to bid someone welcome? My anguish increased with every moment. It seemed as if I was leaving the real world.

Along different stretches of road, two rows of abandoned cars were lined up, doors open and windows down. They had been left to fate, either along the length of the road or pushed into the ditch, in the same condition as when they were abandoned by their fleeing occupants.

Houses in the suburbs were also empty, seemingly haunted, doors and windows opening onto darkness. In courtyards, as on sidewalks, we saw a wild tangle of abandoned objects—dishes, pots, furniture, gas stoves, refrigerators, and many other items of daily use that had been dumped haphazardly during the escape and pillage. There was not a soul to be found, not a dog, a bird, or even a flower. Even factories and warehouses were devastated and abandoned. This apocalyptic world seemed to have come straight out of a nightmare, as if life had been destroyed, chased by a brutal blast of wind, a supernatural catastrophe.

Suddenly a cry rang out in the van. It was a woman named China, who had recognized her house. Standing up, she called out the names of people close to her—her sister, her mother, her friends . . . Then she sat down, stunned. The vehicle continued on. I had caught a glimpse of a huge residence that still exuded the aura of its previous owner's wealth. Everything remained just as it was at the time of the abandonment. The three openings in the facade opened only on silence. They seemed to have spewed into the courtyard a jumble of household objects that were now partially overgrown by weeds.

The sight was terrifying. Fighting back the fears that assailed us, we turned our eyes to avoid seeing more. We had been taught, during the course of many political education seminars, not to doubt, not to criticize, and not to let our imaginations overtake us.

I tried to convince myself that that night I would be far away, in a peaceful, joyful, warm world surrounded by my husband and children. I wanted to forget this apocalypse as quickly as possible.

The bus soon stopped in the courtyard of a huge building that had been the office of the prime minister in General Lon Nol's government. Everyone climbed out in silence, the bus left, and the iron gates closed.

With the same air of authority used at the airport, Sirin ordered us to settle ourselves into the buildings behind the ministry. Obscene graffiti covered the walls, electrical wires hung everywhere, and heaps of paper lay on the ground. Piled at the far end of one wing were iron beds, which we had to set up in this tangle of garbage.

Someone asked how long we would have to stay in this location. The reply: "That will depend on how fast you develop your ideological and political conscience. One month, two months, maybe longer. . . ."

The head of the group warned us that it was forbidden to climb to the top floor and onto the terrace, to run along the enclosure walls, or to make noise that could be heard from outside. We had to stay in a group in the area between the two buildings and watch out for mines and booby-trap grenades.

We divided up the accommodations. Families moved into the small offices, while bachelors assembled in the large rooms. Once the first arrangements were made, we regrouped in the little courtyard. It was there that we saw the arrival of three girls dressed in black: "revolutionary combatants." Everyone gathered to look. It was our first encounter with these heroines about whom we had heard so much and whose battle songs glorified their courage. They were "guerrilla messengers who ran fearlessly through hails of bullets to supply the combatants," "the soldiers of iron will." Willingly and modestly, they rejected the submissive role of the old society in order to take up arms and accomplish great things. We stared at them until they became embarrassed.

The girls carried in dishes and vegetables for the evening meal with the calm, self-controlled movements of peasants. Under the Organization's strict instructions, they refused to respond to our questions and disappeared shortly into what came to be called the kitchen.

In the evening, I was visited by Sirin, who approached me wearing a big grin. I hoped he would announce Sikoeun's imminent arrival, but again my expectations were dashed. He only delivered some worn-out slogans, then boasted about the Khmer revolution's superiority over all previous revolutions, notably because of the abolition of money and the evacuation of the cities' inhabitants to the countryside—resulting in Phnom Penh's becoming a ghost town. I listened patiently to this familiar speech. It was almost identical to the one Sikoeun had used.

In Paris, Sirin had been an active and eager militant. Married with two sons, his house was always open and welcoming. His wife, Vipha, was regarded highly by everyone. Although she belonged to one of the wealthiest families in Battambang Province, for patriotic reasons she had joined the revolution. Intelligent and sensitive, she had become an active and efficient militant. Her mother, who had visited her in Paris just before the events of 1970, had followed her to Peking. Small and plump but not fat, her hair cut very short, Vipha's mother was the image of a true old Khmer woman. In Peking, she had attended all Ieng Sary's lectures, imbibing his words with devotion. At last, after her seventieth year, she had discovered the hidden riches of her country's heritage. She learned, for example, that Mount Aoral is 1,771 meters (5,810 feet) high, a fact that for some reason made her profoundly ecstatic.

She was Buddhist, for which she was respected. Recently, her health had seriously deteriorated, and everyone worried about her worsening condition. But with the news of the victory, the old woman had regained control and, with the strength of a "second wind," flew with us to Phnom Penh.

She was proud of her daughter and son-in-law. She was proud of Angkar for knowing how to liberate her country from foreign domination, even if it cost her all of the wealth her family had accumulated over generations. Most important to her, the future now belonged to her children and her grandchildren.

During the evening meal, Sirin spoke solemnly: "The Organization has chosen to offer you a banquet worthy of the top leaders, prepared with the spirit of self-sacrifice by Kampuchea's heroic combatants. While waiting to join the people to share their joys and sufferings, you are our guests. I hope you realize the honor Angkar is bestowing on you."

In this solemn and stentorian tone, we did not recognize the Sirin from before. One might have thought he was celebrating mass. He continued: "There is no more rice now. It has all been sent to the cooperatives to support the massive reconstruction effort and for the reception of the workers from the cities. But for you, the Organization found rice. The combatants have deprived themselves to be able to offer you this meal. For a long time they have eaten only moldy bread made with rank American flour. . . . Soon, you will have to eat like everybody else. Starting tomorrow, you will eat only two meals, except the children, who will get breakfast."

We wolfed down our last banquet, which consisted of

cabbage soup, sauteed cabbage, rice, and bread. Someone raised the question of the young children's need for fresh vegetables, fruits, milk, sugar . . . More pointed still was the problem of mothers who could not nourish their babies. There were some provisions, but what was to happen when those were used up?

"How to cope?" Sirin retorted. "Well, you will do as the people do! The people's children and babies live well! And their level of revolutionary consciousness is certainly better than yours. Your thoughts demonstrate that Angkar is wise to keep you here. If the people heard you talk like this, they would reject you."

The next day, I woke early. The sky was bright, and I forgot yesterday's worries. This should be a nice place to live, I told myself. Today will be a beautiful day. Surely Sikoeun will come and find us.

Yet the day passed with no further word.

Our position as guests signaled the caution with which Angkar regarded us and the distance it sought to create between the old and the new. The old were those who had fought. Since we arrived *after* the fighting, no matter what our merits, we could never reach their standing.

Meanwhile, people told us we had a huge advantage over those who stayed in France. We were more worthy because we had been indoctrinated in the course of many seminars. That is how the Organization ascribed our roles and challenged us to participate in the race to power. We were under observation while awaiting the joyful day when we would join the people. It was up to each to show his or her talents.

In fact, everyone put themselves to work, restoring the electrical power, washing the windows and tiles, and weeding the lawns.

13

We were also urged to repack our bags and get rid of all impractical objects. Many had kept personal effects, souvenirs, radios, and tape recorders.

"As long as you possess foreign technologies," we were told, "Angkar will give up sending you to the people. The people live without these devices. They live without anything. You have to live like them. The people are good. They have given everything to Angkar, even the children of their own flesh. You must imitate them."

To enter the new society, each of us had to reduce our belongings to a small bundle. Sorting was basic. Few things were fundamentally indispensable. Everything else was assembled in a room to be looked over by the Organization.

This demand, which many had rejected before the departure, was easily satisfied now, and no one complained.

On the evening of the third day, a high revolutionary dignitary visited: Khieu Samphan. He only passed through, surrounded by two bodyguards with guns slung over their shoulders, but his visit underlined the Organization's interest in us. The group leader, "the one responsible for life," as we respectfully referred to him, announced that Angkar was going to organize a seminar dedicated to our political formation. This seminar, to be held on a day still kept secret, would take place in the conference hall of the former ministry. Participants would sleep nearby—in the offices—so that they were always close to their duties in both mind and body. Children would be watched by devoted combatants of high revolutionary awareness.

Strangely, the most sought-after task was cleaning toilets. Khmers are repulsed by fecal matter, and they avert their eyes and change direction as soon as they see any. But given the revolutionary period we were in, overcoming this repugnance was proof of ideological transformation.

The bathrooms overflowed with excrement; the walls were covered with it. It was a splendid occasion to prove one's public spiritedness. Some found hoses, others sponges. The most daring went so far as to clean with their hands and scrape with their nails.

On the upper floor, the offices in the left wing were designated for men, those in the right wing were for nursing women, and former Prime Minister Long Boret's central office was turned into a dormitory for the other women.

The room was huge and luxurious, and I surprised myself by entering on tiptoe. The room was unchanged since the night Phnom Penh fell. Overturned chairs were scattered about in front of a large desk. There was a framed photo of Lon Nol, its glass shattered by a bullet. Papers were strewn all over the floor. People said Long Boret had sat behind his desk waiting for the liberation army, and that with the arrival of the first fighters, he had stood up and extended his hand. But then a struggle had ensued, and the minister had tried to escape by the door behind . . .

I walked over to the little door and opened it apprehensively. The recent past seemed so vivid. I found a narrow spiral stairway and followed it, my heart racing at the thought of stumbling onto the rest of the scene. . . . I found nothing.

Once settled, we were joined in our new quarters by a group of women who had been part of Prince Sihanouk's entourage and who had arrived in Phnom Penh over a month before. The oldest, following tradition, had shaved their heads. We exchanged tales of our experiences.

The fifty beds in our dormitory were arranged in a way that stirred some unhappy memories of boarding school. Falling asleep that night, I felt certain that soon, after the seminar, I would find Sikoeun and we would see better days.

The next morning, everyone assembled piously in the

conference hall and, when Khieu Samphan entered, applauded long and loud. For the occasion we wore new black cotton outfits, which added to the respectful and quasi-religious atmosphere that reigned and made me feel as if I were participating in a secret ceremony.

Seated on the platform, Khieu Samphan looked out at the assembly and then leaned toward his neighbor, Sirin. After whispering in his ear, he rose and left. Sirin spoke and asked us to leave also, which of course everyone did.

After exiting, Sirin approached me and led me aside. Anxiously, dreading something serious about Sikoeun, I listened carefully. He spoke about other subjects for a long time.

"The situation in our country since the April 17 victory is complex," he began. "The American imperialists have never suffered such a radical defeat. China itself has never succeeded in liberating Taiwan. Korea remains divided. And Vietnam owes its victory in large part to the heroic struggle of our people. Without us, they would still be fighting.

"The April 17 triumph is thus a victory of heroic people, with bare hands, over a huge economic, political, and military power. This victory belongs to the Khmer people, and only the Khmer people. . . ."

"Yes, yes," I agreed calmly, while beginning to boil impatiently inside. I saw that everyone was returning to the room and was afraid of being late.

He continued: "Kampuchea and the people of Kampuchea"—"Cambodia" and "the Cambodian people" were no longer used because these terms were considered part of the colonial heritage—"are truly heroic. You know that the people have suffered a great deal under colonialism and French colonialists? The April 17 victory was achieved on our own, do you understand?"

This Cambodian way (or the Khmer Rouge way, at least) of evading the real issue left me feeling helpless.

16

"What am I to understand?"

"During these few days, you are going to take care of your children. If you want, you can take care of other children, too, and later, the Organization will take care of you."

Stung by my exclusion through this unfair ukase, powerless and unable to control my emotions, I turned and left. I collected my things and went to the children's dormitory. A strong smell of urine choked me. Several little ones begged to eat, some had fevers. They were all crying. Their small bodies were covered with oozing mosquito bites. By contrast, the Organization's heroic combatants were sleeping soundly. I changed the wet babies and washed the floor and the linens. The little ones continued to cry.

Ominous premonitions assailed me. What if I had fallen into a trap, if everything I had been told was a lie? I resisted thinking this, but a voice inside me persisted: You are a prisoner, a prisoner. They want to wreak revenge. They want to make you pay a price. My resistance weakened. I had known moments of isolation and doubt and had always stood fast, but this time I cracked. I wept huge tears, those that come when one has suppressed feelings too long. While doing the laundry, I cried all of the tears that were in my body—I was unable to stop.

The two combatants, who had awakened, looked surprised and hurt, ready to recognize their negligence. Still I could not restrain myself. The tears continued to fall in streams. When the wash was done, I hung out the linens. It was a beautiful day—blue sky, sunshine—and that comforted me a little.

In the days that followed, I took care of the children. When their parents emerged between sessions, they pretended not to see me.

During such political education seminars, each person was obliged to give a detailed account of his or her life, actions, and errors, to be accompanied by strong criticism and self-criticism. These seminars had a powerful effect on the participants' spirits. Their minds were molded through an established system of thought control.

I was once again introduced as the intruder and the enemy. I found myself in the same situation as I had been in years before, after Ieng Sary's arrival in Peking. I was Sisyphus at the bottom of the mountain, but I no longer had the desire or the strength needed for a new ascent. The task exceeded my power and certainly did not fit my idea of the role I could play in Cambodia.

When the seminar was over, we returned to our old quarters to await the Organization's decision. Each one returned to his task, keeping his thoughts to himself. Ever conscious of my exclusion, I kept a good distance from my companions and waited for Sikoeun to come.

One night after dinner, in what had become my room, I was watching the girls draw when I heard someone on the stairs. My heart leapt and I felt myself flush. When newly wed and living on the university campus, I had learned to distinguish these footsteps from thousands of others: Sikoeun! With great joy, I threw myself at him. He embraced the three of us; we were all so happy!

I pumped him with questions: Where did he work? What did he do? . . . He didn't answer, in loyalty to the policy of secrecy that, he reminded me, had been a decisive factor in the April 17 victory. I stopped questioning. Nevertheless, I did tell him about my disappointments.

"Have confidence in Angkar," he told me. "Angkar knows better than you what you deserve. It is saving the right place for you."

"Which?"

He didn't answer. Actually, he didn't know anything about it; he only responded the way he had been taught to answer. I knew this, and yet I clung to the notion that the Organization would soon get me out of there and put me to good use.

In fact, shortly thereafter, the Organization, satisfied with the seminar, informed us that everyone would soon join the "base," meaning the peasants.

That same night, a jeep drove into the courtyard. Si-koeun got out. "Angkar sent me to fetch you," he said. "Quickly ready your things. Don't say anything to anybody."

Three minutes later, with my children and my bags, I left without saying good-bye to a single one of my companions.

· *Two* ·

The jeep drove through the gate, slipped onto what had been a boulevard, proceeded not more than fifty meters, and stopped in a courtyard. It was a dark night. We got out and followed Sikoeun, who moved easily in the dark. We crossed a hall, which led to another courtyard, walked along a wall, and finally arrived at a small, lighted room. A figure came toward us: it was Krean Lean.

A former student in Moscow, Krean Lean had taken sides with Sihanouk in Peking after the coup d'état. He was named chief of staff under Penn Nouth and then, having expressed a desire to join the resistance, underwent a period of political education. In January 1973, when the Americans were undertaking massive bombings of the country, he was with a group of fifteen intellectuals sent to the liberated zones. The resistance had made him a powerful man.

"We have just learned of your arrival," he said. "The combatants are preparing a banquet for you. When you drop off your things, everything will be ready."

This warm welcome heartened me, and I all but forgot the past three painful, uncertain weeks.

To get to the living quarters, we had to cross, in the dark, a narrow passage littered with abandoned trucks. We felt our way to avoid being hurt.

The living space was on the first floor. Sikoeun had already installed his bed in what had been a kitchen. The girls and I put our things in another room. A third room was unoccupied. The toilets were at the end of the hall.

We had an iron bed for three and a dresser in our room. An American calendar, opened to April, hung behind the door, a last souvenir of the previous occupants. Each day had been carefully crossed out. *Rains* was written in on April 10—probably the first rain of the monsoon, earlier than usual. The word *nothing* was entered on the eleventh. The twelfth had been crossed out, and after that: nothing. Had an American lived in this room until the last days before a precipitous exit from Phnom Penh? I tried to imagine the person. Had he been big, blond? Had he been afraid?

Once again I had the sensation of being projected into the recent past. The war was still present. I could feel the vibrations of history.

"Angkar is bestowing a big honor on you by permitting you to stay here," Sikoeun told me.

The banquet table was laden with a kettle of soup, plates of fried food, rice, bread, sugar, and banana fritters. All of this demonstrated warm hospitality.

During the meal, Krean Lean talked about various subjects. Listening to him, I had the same strange feeling that I had felt in seeing Sirin. His behavior was so studied, his stereotyped expressions borrowed directly from the official line of Ieng Sary and the other leaders.

Pompously, he recalled the sacrifices and heroism of the fighters of the people's combatants. He spoke of his attachment and devotion to Angkar, who he said had been his real father and mother, and toward the people whom he tried to serve with all his heart and all his power.

He told us that when he had been deathly ill, a poor peasant had given him his only worldly possession, a chicken. He claimed that the sacrifice had hastened his recuperation.

Following the secrecy orders, I made sure not to ask him about our mutual friends. Yet I would have liked to know what had happened to Kamanh, Varith, and Padet, all of whom had joined the resistance and, I hoped, returned to Phnom Penh.

At the end of the meal, Krean Lean asked me: "What are you going to call yourself?"

In the ranks of combatants, everyone was required to change his name. But I didn't expect to be affected, so I was taken by surprise.

"You could call yourself Phâl," Sikoeun suggested. *Phâl* means "fruit," or "harvest." The term suited me. "It is very good," I said, and thought, May my work be crowned with success.

Knowing how Cambodians excel in the art of making up names, I was convinced that it was not by chance that the chosen name included my initials.

We stood up from the table. My Khmer baptism had just been completed.

Returning to my "place of rest," I found several young combatants busily fixing up a mosquito net. "Hello," I said.

They lifted their heads but didn't respond. Clearly, I was very gauche! Just as everyone had discontinued hand shaking and question asking, it was no longer in good taste to say hello. I would have to get used to it.

When my daughters came to be with me, the combatants played with them, embracing them, teasing them, and spanking their little round behinds. The Khmer tokens of affection were very different from the Chinese. The little ones were surprised by the attention, but they said nothing. I tried to communicate with the combatants and again asked their names. They replied very shyly. But little by little, their tongues loosened. They were ecstatic about my daughters, who reminded them of the little sisters they had left behind when they joined Angkar.

When I was alone, I arranged my things and questioned myself about my new home. The frame supporting the mosquito netting strangely resembled antennas. Were we perhaps in the neighborhood of a radio station?

Late that night, Sikoeun woke me up. "Come quickly," he said. "There is an urgent task."

He briefly explained that Ieng Sary was leaving the next day for Bangkok and a press communiqué he was taking needed to be translated. He said this job was a sign of Angkar's confidence in me. I quickly did the translation, dissecting each expression and weighing each word, as is done in political translating and as I had learned in China.

Sikoeun, seated nearby in order to "assist" me, exclaimed, "You have made progress!"

"I still have many shortcomings," I replied. But inside I was very pleased.

Yet the next day Krean Lean announced that I would be working in the kitchen at B1. I was disappointed. I had dreamed of an outdoor job, but instead I would be confined to an old automobile repair shop built of blackened planks on hard-packed ground. It was no place to watch over children. Furthermore, I knew nothing about cooking, although given the scarcity of supplies, the meals were invariably made up of soup and a piece of bread. The bread was made in town; despite its grayish color, it was fairly good. A little truck delivered it every other day. The daily ration was 450 grams per person.

At eight in the morning, the two combatants who worked in the kitchen were already energetically preparing lunch, chopping up a gourd and a chunk of fish and throwing the pieces into a pot of boiling water. By eight-thirty, everything was cooked. They quickly set the table, then covered the dishes and food with a piece of netting before putting the drinking water on to boil.

"Why such haste?" I asked them.

"We are afraid of being late."

The one who responded could not have been more than fifteen or sixteen years old. She had a beautiful watch, but she did not know how to use it. "Everyone has one," she explained to me. "Angkar distributed them. They are all over Phnom Penh."

I decided to teach them how to read the face and tell time. But that assumed that they already knew how to add and subtract, which they did not. I felt guilty about introducing them to the infernal mechanism that measures the passage of time.

At eleven o'clock, everyone assembled around the three tables: one for the boys, one for the girls, one for my daughters and me. The men and women working for what I learned was the Ministry of Foreign Affairs were very young. They ranged from seventeen to twenty. The girls came from the northern province of Preah Vihear. Scarcely taller than five feet, they were nevertheless strongly built. In contrast to the slender, fragile Phnom Penh women, they had square, fleshy faces, flat noses, big almond eyes rimmed with black, very thin waists, high chests, and strong arms. Everything in them bespoke the Apsaras—the celestial dancers in the bas-reliefs of the Angkor temples. They had simple, regal smiles that radiated strength, modesty, and wisdom.

In the canteen, people spoke with one another quietly. Once the meal was over, each person took his or her plate and spoon, washed them in basins set out for this purpose, and placed them on the drying rack. After drinking a big cup of boiled water, they departed.

The community that welcomed me reflected, I was told, the new society where people preached poverty, the renunciation of worldly belongings, the use of only a single garment, austere eating habits, and a communal and fraternal life. I was seduced by this ideal of life and the hopes it seemed to bring. I wished for a world where social relations excluded competition, jealousy, greed—where simplicity and impoverishment would put an end to the aggression and tension created by the desire to possess. I dreamed of a society where honor no longer fell to the greediest but rather to the most devoted and unselfish. I aspired to a truth without dispute, which no religion or system of thought had yet given humankind.

Soon I undertook to explore my new lodging. The building had three stories and was covered with grillwork that enclosed it like a birdcage. This protection had been designed by the former American occupants to ward off hand grenade attacks. Amid the rubble strewn on the ground around the building were many musical instruments— even a piano, which lorded over the junk, bags of sand, empty bottles, and rolls of barbed wire.

We were installed in what had once been the Academy of Fine Arts, according to the still-legible inscription on a dusty truck covered with pine needles and abandoned in the courtyard.

On either side of the building stood several low structures that appeared to have been a dance hall and two village halls. A vast, fallow field of manioc extended from there, bordered by private residences. Finally, on the other side of the boulevard stood the building we had walked through upon our arrival. It was a huge, contoured building adorned with large bay windows. Under the main entrance one could read the inscription: "Presidence du Conseil." The interior had been torn apart by a bomb, revealing pieces of twisted beams through the gaping holes.

What had been a pleasant garden now served as a dump. There lay helter-skelter amid the fine red gravel a washing machine, a sewing machine, shelves, cabinets, and an old moped used by the cooks. A pool of stagnant water had formed in a bomb crater; it stank so much that even the ducks refused to go near it. Near the entrance, the bodies of two soldiers had been discovered.

In the middle of the courtyard was a basketball court. The workshop at the far end had been transformed into a kitchen. Farther out, a fallow area gave way to the usual apocalyptic landscape containing everything from dented pots and pans and damaged furniture to twisted television antennas. The town was enveloped in a strange silence that was anguished, tense, and vibrant. It evoked in me the image of Guernica: pain, distress, suffering. I could almost hear those agonized cries.

On the ground floor of the council, I found a little room filled with precious objects—delicately sculpted statues, silver platters, crystal glasses, a porcelain service, and ivory tusks—that had been collected and, while awaiting better use, stored by the combatants. My daughters were dazzled by the treasures of this Ali Baba cave, and the following morning installed themselves to prepare a sumptuous tea party. I caught them in mid-play. Narén, the oldest, was painstakingly dragging a crystal ice bucket filled with soil, while her little sister Sokha was making little cakes with moka teacups and finely chiseled liqueur glasses.

I could barely resist exploding with laughter. If their father could only see them now! He wanted to make them real revolutionaries, while they seemed more interested in the lives of princesses!

The first days in our new home were spent waiting. Kitchen work hardly filled my hours, and I had not been approached for other duties since the translation that first night. The morning fast left my brain empty and my legs shaky until lunch.

As I rested one morning under a tree, Sikoeun sat down next to me. He seemed unhappy.

27

"While throughout the country, the people are hard at work, you sit there doing nothing."

Furious at his attitude, I responded, "I am waiting for someone to give me work to do."

"You could sweep the basketball court," he offered.

There was only one old broom to sweep this huge area, which was surrounded by cypress, so I asked Sikoeun for a more efficient tool. He lost his temper: "Do you think the people have brooms? They only have their hands. With their bare hands the combatants beat the biggest imperialist power in the world. . . ."

Once again our relationship took a difficult turn. Finally reunited, we were once again splitting apart. Sikoeun spied on me, criticized me, judged me. I felt he was tormented with fear.

In mid-November, Ri, my old neighbor at the Friendship Hotel in Peking, rejoined us. Ri had been placed with Prince Sihanouk's entourage, which Angkar had sent to different parts of the country. Just as she was about to board the truck to leave with her children, she was informed that she must stay in Phnom Penh. She watched with anguish as her children disappeared toward some unknown destination.

Ri was a woman of the world. She had once been one of the ten most fashionable women of Phnom Penh. With bitterness, nobility, and simplicity, she now lived like everyone else. She dressed in black, wore no makeup, and, at the common table, ate soups that in the past she would not have fed to her dog.

Our fates were tied. At the Ministry of Foreign Affairs offices in Phnom Penh, where we were forced to stay, we were not given any real work. It seemed to us that their intent was to keep us from having contact with the people. We found this unjust. But our complaints were met with:

"Angkar knows how to judge people according to their value," and "The Organization has in mind projects for you which you will be told about when the time is right."

Ri stayed in the room across from me, and, loyal to her tastes, she put up some decorations on her walls. "It can't bother anyone," she said to me. "This is *my* place."

That, however, was a misjudgment of the scrutiny Angkar accorded us. The next day we were moved; we had to cart beds, dressers, and bags to the next floor. Two days later, we were asked to return to our old rooms, which we did patiently. Then we had to change wings and shortly thereafter return to the starting point . . . Rebuffed at every turn, Ri finally abandoned her decorative murals, and we were no longer bothered.

Despite these vexations, we did not give up trying to bring a little order to our living space. We collected and organized all of the medical supplies—all kinds of antibiotics from unknown origins—that littered the scene. Fortifying tonics, on the other hand, had disappeared, their sweet, acidic taste having been appreciated by the combatants entering Phnom Penh.

After arranging the items for medical use, we tried to clean up the surrounding area by demolishing the props built here and there, removing the barbed-wire fences, and dismantling the sandbag walls. We amused ourselves with our daring and found ourselves far more hardy than we had imagined.

In Phnom Penh, I met another acquaintance, Seila, whom I had known in Peking, where he had been Khieu Samphan's interpreter during his August 1975 visit. Seila had been a brilliant intellectual—living proof that the Khmer revolution was not only an insurrection of peasants.

Every day at four-thirty in the afternoon, Seila came to water the vegetables being grown in ridges of soil brought from the park above. He slipped along quickly under his yoke, pumping water from a nearby stream and emptying it onto his turnips. He made no fewer than fifteen trips to complete his daily task.

One day Seila and a companion, to whom he gave the task of bringing soil for the new furrows from the field of manioc, confided to us, "We need twenty banks of soil. The windy month has arrived. There is no time to lose."

"We are going to help you," I told him, only too happy to devote myself, at last, to working the soil, as I had dreamed of doing.

We unearthed some containers and an American spade and put ourselves to work. We had just started when Sikoeun appeared. In a falsely detached tone, he asked, "Is there nothing left to be done in the kitchen?"

My heart skipped a beat. I answered harshly: "What's the matter? What do you want? Talk honestly for once."

Indicating with a gesture the old park that we were transforming, he said: "This garden belongs to the people in the offices. It is up to them to do the work."

"And so? Time is of the essence. How can we provide for our needs if we don't plant vegetables?"

The argument was irrefutable. Sikoeun finally admitted his real concern: "We could see you from the road. There are Chinese who pass occasionally . . . and Angkar comes and goes!"

Refusing to argue any further, we tried to be discreet and pursued our work. We improved productivity by using a wheelbarrow found in a corner. This enabled us to carry a basket and two pots of soil on each trip. One pulled while the other pushed, with the children also taking part. We all felt we were participating in one of the great Asiatic construction projects popularized by the media. I was very happy in this antlike role.

Shovelful after shovelful, trip after trip, we made quick progress in our project. Seila uncovered cabbage plants of all kinds: Chinese and Japanese, white and green, long and round, which he planted as he went along. The turnips, benefiting from the monsoon blowing from the north, grew gloriously. The garden was bursting into bloom.

November, the windy month, is the time for oranges. Many were trucked in every two or three days. The cooperatives in Battambang, said to be conscious of the sacrifices of the Phnom Penh combatants, sent loads of this precious fruit as a sign of gratitude.

This was the first time since our arrival that we had fruit. After the meal, we filled our containers with oranges and in small groups retired to a shady corner to, as we called it jokingly, "open a work site." Following the example of the combatants, each day I consumed quite a few oranges. Unfortunately, this excessive ingestion of fruit triggered in me a fierce intestinal inflammation. Sick and weakened, I lost my ardor for work, for which Sikoeun did not fail to notice and reproach me.

"Watch out," he said one night, "people are calling you *smock smanh*." ("*Smock smanh*, spirit in confusion," was a Buddhist term adopted as revolutionary phraseology. It meant: "You don't give to your work any more; you are not in harmony with your companions" and thus "you oppose Angkar.")

"Who says that?" I asked.

Without responding, Sikoeun continued: "Your country owes a debt of blood to our people. For a hundred years, the French colonists, your ancestors, plundered us. And that is why, today, life is so difficult here. You are the only French person here. You have a unique opportunity to give meaning to your life. But French arrogance stifles you. You need to be taught revolutionary modesty."

I remained perplexed during this speech. Once again I asked myself what attitudes and plans the Khmer community and the Organization had in mind for me.

One night after dinner, Sikoeun invited us to visit "Granny-cakes." I willingly got my daughters ready, relishing the thought of biting into a sweet delicacy.

Yey, or Granny-cakes, was sitting with two young assistants in a little house just a hundred meters from the village halls. She was in charge of making pastries for our special guests and foreign residents. Small and chunky, her gray hair cut short, she looked like everyone's good mother cake maker. However, upon our arrival, she settled into the shadow-darkened room.

"I am infinitely grateful to Angkar," Granny said, "for the task assigned to me reflecting great confidence. At my age, I couldn't hope for a better way to contribute to the building of the country."

Sikoeun replied in a similar tone of icy rhetoric, while I withdrew in an attitude of waiting and of revolutionary modesty.

Turning to the girls, Granny said: "I have no more cakes tonight. Nothing here belongs to me; the flour, sugar, and eggs are provided by the Organization. Everything is rationed. I send the cakes I make away."

We left a bit saddened. But later I would frequently have the opportunity to visit Granny to help relieve her rheumatism with my acupuncture needles. The first time I saw her, she offered me a cake. I thought it was a test, perhaps directed by Angkar, so I declined politely. After that, she acted naturally.

At the end of my visits, I learned that Yey was originally from Battambang. She had married young and had had three children in rapid succession while the war was at its height. Her husband had joined the underground, where he served as head of the region. To provide for her family, Yey had started making and selling cakes.

After the Geneva Conference, her husband had returned

and they'd had happy days together. But the repression swept down on the former leaders of the underground and Yey, with her children, had to go into exile. She settled in China and was joined by her husband. Her daughters studied medicine and her son became an engineer, which was a great source of pride for her.

Then the war began anew, and in 1972, after her husband's death, Yey and her children joined the new underground on the Ho Chi Minh Trail. Her girls joined Angkar and her son joined the army. He was killed during one of the terrible bombings of 1973.

"I learned about his death six months later," she said without skipping a beat. "Many others died like him on the front line. He sacrificed himself for victory. Today, he is here, near me, around us, present in our action and in our thoughts, in our hopes which are finally coming to fruition."

Yey cast all of her words and all of her thoughts in the Angkar mold. Her role as mother merged with her life as militant.

Her face lit up only when she talked about Krous, her daughter Nane's little boy. Born in the far northeast during the war, the baby had contracted a high fever from which, for most, there was no escape. But, while a shroud had already been prepared for him, he had survived. He was afflicted, however, with a large swelling on the left side of his body.

At the end of 1975, while the toddler was taking his first steps, the worst came to pass. With each passing day, his face stiffened and his steps became more labored.

Yey cherished this child, condemned to such a profound handicap. She talked to him constantly, played with him, and hugged him while humming sweet melodies. Through his laughs and mischievousness, Krous brought much joy to his grandmother. Through their song of love, Yey and Krous brightened the revolutionary universe of B1.

At the beginning of December, the coconut trees around the parks bore their fruit, each one with a cluster or two of coconuts—still green, the way they are savored in Cambodia. The oranges were already forgotten and the soup toward the end of the year was very thin. That is why we all looked longingly upon these fruits filled with a milk reputed to be nourishing. Everyone salivated just looking at them, and some couldn't resist handling them in passing. Unfortunately, it was forbidden to pick them.

One morning, Seila could not resist climbing and taking several, which he then made us taste. It was delicious. My daughters took such pleasure in it that the next day I saw them conscientiously weeding the garden. Their efforts, of course, were not disinterested ones, and they did not escape Seila, either. He gave in to their appeals—in which Chinese was mixed with Khmer—and resolved to pick a few more. We sat in a circle and prepared to feast, when I suddenly saw Seila turn beet red, jump up, and go back to work. I turned around to catch a glimpse of an Angkar jeep parked in the courtyard.

Ieng Sary did not reveal his presence, but soon thereafter, Seila was transferred.

· *Three* ·

Khmer as we spoke it among the ranks was different from the Khmer taught and used up to the present. It had shed its old skin. While the academic language contained a plethora of Sanskrit and Pali words, making it difficult to understand, the new way of writing was less complex and the new spoken language greatly simplified.

Changes affected the vocabulary and levels of language. The old was extremely hierarchical, mirroring the society, to the point that such commonly used words as *I*, *eat*, and *sleep* had three different expressions, depending on the person to whom one spoke—whether peasant, valet, prince, bonze, or citizen—as well as one's own position.

For *eat*, the peasant word *haup* had been kept, and the citizen's *niam* henceforth was cause for laughter. *Rest* was preferable to *sleep*, in keeping with the value placed on the difference between sleep and rest. The words *husband* and *wife* were abolished in favor of the more general *family*, with its peasant resonance. When talking about a child, one no longer used the word *vear*, weighted as it was with pejorative meaning, but the pronoun *koat*, before used only for adults.

Among the innovations in usage was the replacement of *solicit* by *suggest*. One now said: *I suggest your hoe* instead of *Lend me your hoe*. This nuance, difficult to translate,

35

forcefully highlighted the end of the time when the lender or usurer reigned over the peasants and the poor.

Hello, how are you? was abandoned for, literally, *Are you content and tranquil?* or *Are you free of all fever?* which corresponded better to daily preoccupations. *Thank you, excuse me,* and *please,* disappeared from current use.

There was also a curious usage for the words *ration, support,* and *open.* Each allotment of clothes, sandals, food, medicine, and so forth was described as the *opening of a ration.* So, for example, Angkar *opened* a shirt, while the beneficiary was *supported* by Angkar with a shirt. Individuals were officially prohibited from exchanging gifts.

This transformation of language assumed new social behavior and was supposed to lead to respect and equality among all. That is how *I* also disappeared from the spoken language, underlining the primacy of the collective over the individual. One would speak or act only in the name of the group: *we* do this, *we* think that . . . This substitution of *we* for *I,* in the name of abolishing all individualism, was well assimilated by simple workers, but it was used by cadres to create confusion.

The Ministry of Foreign Affairs saw the size of its seminars increasing noticeably toward the end of 1975.

One morning, dozens of young combatants arrived at B1 in little groups in single file. They had just attended a political seminar, and they had the serious air of people expecting to carry out big responsibilities. All had put on their best black clothes.

The seminar lasted several days and we learned that participants had come from B2, B4, B6, and elsewhere. (Each administrative unit had a numbered letter—*B* stood for foreign affairs, *K* for defense, *P* for hospital, and so on—and was directed by one of Angkar's leaders: Ieng Sary, Ieng Thirith, Son Sén, Vorn Vet, and others.)

36

Custom would have it that during a seminar, food was more plentiful. A van brought in fish, vegetables, and fresh-water lobster the size of an arm.

The seminars discussed the new situation in Cambodia. They covered themes I knew well: the clairvoyance of Angkar, the evacuation of towns, the abolition of money. "The Cambodian revolution is without historical precedent," "It settles the eternal contradiction between town and country," "Angkar surpasses Lenin and goes further than Mao," "The whole world turns its eyes toward Cambodia because its revolution is the most beautiful and the most pure."

After these meetings, Angkar also tried to explain the role given to Prince Sihanouk. Sihanouk, who had been presented as the prime enemy of the people, had become, after the coup d'état against Lon Nol, the ally of the Khmer Rouge. This reversal—or "compromise"—had not always been well understood by the combatants.

"It is a political compromise," Angkar insisted. "As long as Sihanouk is our ally, he is no longer on the side of the enemy. Sihanouk is our hostage. We can do with him what we want. At the United Nations, he works for us. We have put the lion in its cage."

By the end of the year, the manpower at B1 had almost tripled. The dining hall had become too small, so the village hall was used instead. The kitchen was located near the new cafeteria, in a hut built especially for this purpose. Better fitted out, this kitchen contained three hearths instead of just one.

Among the newcomers, some of the work force was devoted to raising produce for greater self-sufficiency. One group of young women set out to clear an old manioc field. I left our vegetable plot to join them temporarily. Mingling with members of their collective movement, I found myself surprised by its homogeneity and efficiency. We advanced in a straight line, buoyed up by the group.

The individual was absorbed, even transported, by the members as a whole, to the point where the group became a necessity. Not once did any girl strike off on her own, even to find water.

We stopped frequently. During these pauses, as during the work, these people talked profusely—unless overcome by the desire to sing. They had beautiful voices and impressive memories. They remembered melodies heard only once and passed on the words of multiple couplets, carefully copied into school notebooks.

I felt good among these young women, who were simple but willing and determined, young but already mature. They accepted me without hesitation, and that gave me a simple joy and justification for having come to Cambodia.

Among the new arrivals were a number of cadres from the underground called *bang*, which is to say the older ones, the "grands." They settled in abandoned villas and on the floors of still-unoccupied, fenced-off houses.

The first to arrive was Môm. He allowed his white shirt, which he wore beneath a black vest, to be ironed elegantly, and he sprayed himself generously with a fragrant cologne—hardly in keeping with the official profile of an Angkar cadre doing manual labor and leading a simple life. Seeing me, Môm exclaimed: "Here is the Norman Bethune of Kampuchea!" (Norman Bethune was a Canadian surgeon who, during the war of resistance against the Japanese, had lent aid to the Communist Chinese. He died from a fever and was elevated by them to the rank of international hero.)

Then Nou arrived holding an infant, accompanied by her son Phneou and her husband Saev. She settled at Granny-cakes's with her children.

A little later, Tho and Moeun, a young couple, arrived with their little daughter Pech ("diamond"), followed by three older couples, Cheang and Touch, Yôm and Din, and their five children, ranging from three to seventeen years. Yaêm and Ni, with three children, also joined us. All were accompanied by bodyguards and carried trunks, suitcases, and other containers whose contents Ri and I speculated about.

The elders were venerated, but they surprised us by their unusual behavior, the value of their luggage, and the personnel attached to their service.

One day, Ri caught the bodyguards searching through Yôm and Yaêm's things. "What right do you have to search through my things while I am working?" Ri protested.

"It seems you did not turn everything over to Angkar," she was told.

Din, Yom's wife, had an aide-de-camp named Li whom she ordered around.

"Li, come here, Li, go there!" could be heard constantly. Din used him as a servant. Li carried out her orders quickly and quietly, and still his matron took every opportunity to snub him: "Comrade Li, did you not hear what I just told you? You are lacking in revolutionary work zeal! Be careful, comrade, not to stray from the just line and to show yourself worthy of the ideology Angkar has given you!"

Yom was very proud of his wife. "Before the revolution," he would say, "she was an ill-tempered housewife. She ran her kitchen in every sense but without putting a foot in it." But Angkar educated Din and gave her the responsibility of district head. The revolution had totally transformed her.

During the day, the elders often explored abandoned houses. They returned with bric-a-brac and clothes, more or less valuable, which they pretended they were sending to the cooperatives. But one day I caught them discussing how much money they might get for a load of precious stones they had just found . . .

In the kitchen, despite the poverty, special foods arrived for the elders. Small portions were Angkar's custom, but often they were supplemented by banquets of chicken, pork, wine, and sticky rice, which were served in their rooms. Every morning for breakfast, bodyguards went to fetch fresh white bread baked especially for foreign residents.

Settling the elders in B1 signaled a reorganization of the occupants of the camp. Inhabitants were assembled into distinct groups according to their rank and period of service in the resistance. The oldest took the best for themselves and sent the "less evolved" to individual villas.

That is how we came to move to a villa that once belonged to Bopha Devi, one of Sihanouk's daughters and a premier dancer, before sheltering the offices of the Thai embassy. While cleaning it, we found a case full of Thai currency as well as a stash of grenades.

A dozen of us shared this princely dwelling. The children, Sikoeun, and I shared one big room on the ground floor, with an adjoining bathroom. It wasn't so bad.

One brisk December morning, I was surprised to see my old friend Catherine come to B1. Following revolutionary orders, she had sacrificed her magnificent hair. Catherine, whose mother was French, was the daughter of Prasith, the fourth son in the large Thiounn family. We had become friends when she came to Peking in 1972 to study medicine.

She recounted how the Khmer students in China—about fifty students of medicine—had come to Phnom Penh the previous month. Well received, they had been invited to attend a seminar before all were sent to the countryside—except for Catherine. She could not understand this decision, which pained and surprised her. We supposed one needed to be of pure Khmer stock to merit being sent out among the peasants.

Now called Pheap, she was a friendly person who, having now shared her grief, regained her usual gaiety and dynamism. We made a happy couple. The manual work, mixing soil and garbage, cutting wood, or watering vegetables, seemed more a vacation than an expiation of our French intellectual past.

Soon Pheap was accepted by all of the young women combatants and was admitted to the evening meetings. According to Khieu Samphan, these evening gatherings —literally, "life sessions"—were to be "a daily accounting of revolutionary activities," a daily ritual essential to mobilizing the spirit. At this gathering, all of the chores were listed. Each action, every thought, had to be applied to the current revolutionary slogans. Thus, in this time of "working hard to revitalize the economy," "counting on one's own forces," and "denying one's own needs in order to bring a surplus to Angkar," one could hear the president of the meeting say: "These past few days, we have raised five ridges of soil and planted one hundred cabbages. Unfortunately, some seedlings did not take root because they were burned by the sun. The straw hats laid down to protect them were blown away by the wind. Therefore, we must find other plants. This will take time and energy which we can't give to the revitalization of the economy."

One volunteer would seize the opportunity for self-criticism: "Respected president, respected comrades! Concerning what you just heard, I want to stress that the insufficient yields from the plantings of the cabbages are due to a lack of revolutionary vigilance and sense of responsibility on our part. It is a serious fault because it compromises our subsistence and contribution to Angkar."

Then, raising his voice, he would conclude: "We are determined to enforce our revolutionary vigilance. We are determined to remedy our shortcomings and to work hard at the country's economic recovery. We are determined to submerge our own needs and to give our surplus to Angkar."

Two or three more would speak up, embellishing the same theme, each resolving to do better the next day than he or she had done the day before.

Or else someone would bring up conflicts that had arisen between combatants.

At noon one day, I did not eat well. The soup was cold and had nothing in it. My head was spinning all afternoon and I had little energy for work and the revolution.

"Respected president, respected comrades!" growled the cook, aroused. "We lack vegetables and meat and we don't do all we could to improve daily conditions for all to give them the energy needed for national reconstruction. We have shortcomings and we are determined to correct them, but we point out that the comrade arrived late and many arrived early. Furthermore, there are too many comrades who take more than they should without thinking of others. They only see their own interest to the detriment of the general good."

Someone else tried to outdo him: "We should think about the peasants in the cooperatives who lack so much and who, despite everything, deprive themselves to uphold Angkar, those who work day and night to build ditches and dig canals."

They arrived then at an agreement that everyone should arrive on time. They also named someone to serve the soup.

It was, in fact, a way of airing dirty laundry occasionally. Life would then go on with its strict rules, timetables, and restrictions. The young, coming from peasant families of ancient traditions, accepted this discipline with good humor.

Despite my difficulties with collective living, I had to admit that it had the great advantage of freeing the work force, which was appreciable in this postwar period. Daily life was improved by it. It took just three people to handle the provisions and cooking for a hundred others. With some fish and a big basket of fresh vegetables, these three made a soup for everybody.

Of course, all of this implied a great deal of tolerance and understanding on the part of each individual and a great deal of devotion by the cooks. But during this period, goodwill and solidarity ruled. The ambiance was good and life was agreeable, despite the many shortages.

Allowing that we were now living in the hardest of times, we were told: "The situation will improve quickly and the collectivist regime will progress." Everyone was convinced of it.

The bread, kneaded with moldy flour, had become inedible, and it was with great relief that, at the end of December (instead of January, as predicted), it was replaced with new rice. Each of us thanked Angkar from the bottom of his stomach, and our hearts, recharged, now fully supported renewed propaganda. "Long live Angkar!" "Long live the economic line!" "Long live collectivization!" "Develop the country in great strides!" we heard from all sides. And we joined in chorus: "Let's advance in huge bounds toward the development of our country!"

With the last moon of the year, an icy north wind began to blow. I never dreamed it could be so cold in a tropical country. In the morning, on the piece of land we were clearing, we built a fire which we fed with manioc and potato roots. It felt good.

Christmas coincided with my second daughter's birthday. Since our departure from France, I had stopped celebrating festivals and anniversaries. Both the Khmer community and the sacrilegious universe of the cultural revolution that had raged in Peking had divorced me from

43

these familial ceremonies. I was engulfed in the drift of daily life, but on this Christmas, 1975, it was cold and I was in the mood to warm our hearts and our bodies.

Sokha turned three. Her little round face with its clear complexion looked so pretty, like an iridescent pearl above her black outfit. She never complained about deprivation or loneliness. Instead, she took refuge in another world, which she unveiled for us in fantastic stories. A wonderful world where birds talked and flowers danced. A world colored the rose of sunrise, populated by generous elders, and removed in time and space from our present reality.

I had nothing to give my daughters. I ferreted around like a cat in search of sustenance, but in vain. In despair, I took the girls to Granny-cakes, hoping she would understand. She was just making some delicacies with egg yolk cooked in syrup. Unfortunately, Yey could not manage her stock of cakes as her heart would have wanted. We settled for the warmth of the wood fire and the sweet smell of cooking syrup.

Identical days followed each other, without Sundays or holidays, punctuated only by the gong whose shrill ring called us to rise at five-thirty in the morning and again at both mealtimes.

We got up early and went to bed late, completely dressed.

Five minutes after waking, we were already watering the vegetable gardens. From somewhere, we always heard buckets clanking, voices, and the sound of water splashing on the vegetables. We swept the courtyard. At sunrise, everything was clean and in order.

New Year's Day arrived without fireworks or joy. I felt sure that in my family, sparkling glasses were being raised to us, the absent ones. After three months in Phnom Penh, I had heard no news from home and had had no chance to send any letters.

On the night of January 4, Sikoeun came back from the office earlier than usual. Carrying a dossier, he approached me and solemnly put his hand on my elbow. After a silence, he said: "In inviting you this evening to witness this exceptional document, Angkar is demonstrating great confidence in you. It is a secret, a great state secret, a historic document for the nation and the people of Kampuchea, as well as for all of humanity."

Sikoeun was taking great pleasure in testing my curiosity. I was careful not to demonstrate any impatience. He continued: "Now that the people have food to eat, Angkar is working to solve affairs of state. The new Kampuchea will soon celebrate its first anniversary. It needs a name, a government, and a constitution. Here is the future constitution. I brought it this evening so you can translate it."

I modestly took the document and set out to do my best. Sikoeun put his hand on my head and made me bow softly. It was a way he had of expressing his tenderness.

"It is very short," Sikoeun said. "A real model. Completely the opposite of those that govern the so-called Western or popular democracies."

After scanning it, I launched into an attempt at translation. The expressions and hallowed phrases escaped me, however; being removed from the thinking of the document's authors, I could not master the subject. It cost me in harsh remonstrances: "She is French but incapable of writing in good French! Her heart refuses to serve the people of Kampuchea!"

On January 8, the radio broadcast the death of Chou En-lai. I went to alert Pheap. We knew that for China this marked the loss of one who was loved by all, and we shared the sadness of the Chinese friends we had made earlier.

Life went on around us. The young carried out their work in total oblivion. The office workers pursued their routine in a thoroughly joyous manner, while the elders evinced a frank satisfaction. "We have to watch out for China," they said. "We certainly owe China a lot, and it is a great country, but it wants to make us its satellite."

It was then that I received my first letter from my mother. My joy was as great as the length of the wait. Her letter was very warm. She talked about what everybody was doing. She also wrote a glowing paragraph on Angkar—with the censors in mind, no doubt. Finally, she encouraged me to carry on.

After rereading her letter several times, I felt ashamed of my weaknesses and doubts. I had sought out this experience, and I owed it to myself to persevere.

Sikoeun let me know that I had authorization to write back. I wrote a long letter filled with details. I did not mention the privations or the strange behavior of Angkar and its cadres. "The people had to have been very close to Angkar and conscious of their responsibilities to carry off the April 17 victory," I wrote, knowing that, unfortunately, she would not understand that I meant that Angkar cadres were not at the peak of their victory!

In essence, I wrote a piece of propaganda. I gave my letter to Sikoeun. Two weeks later, he brought it back, saying, "All is well."

"If all is well," I said, "why has it not been sent?"

Sikoeun sighed. He was always at a loss in response to my quick reactions and my French manner. He suggested that I take back certain words and ideas, so that the letter would be "interpreted as an Angkar command." I categorically refused. Rather than fight about it, he chose to reproach me: "Ah, if only my wife had been Cambodian!"

In this strange world of hope and violence, Sikoeun and I tried to find our way as a couple. Founded on the ideal of "tomorrows that sing," and then shattered into a million pieces by Khmer chauvinism, our union worked for a while, but communication was not easy. Reasons of state ranked higher than affairs of the heart.

One night, as I read by the light of a little lamp, swathed in a coverlet to protect myself from mosquitoes, Sikoeun brought me a big glass of coffee. He knew how much I liked coffee, and he smiled, showing that he was glad to be able to make me happy. I relished a sip. How good it tasted!

Triumphant, Sikoeun announced, "It is coffee from Pailin!"

Clearly, he couldn't pass up such a splendid opportunity to cite the merits of his country.

"The coffee of Pailin is great!" I replied.

During the course of the conversation that followed, Sikoeun confessed to me, very gently, that once, during the resistance, he had contemplated marrying a compatriot.

"You understand," he said, "I was far from you and the children, all alone. . . ."

I smiled. For me, this confession confirmed what I had suspected at his departure.

"I would have married her," he continued, "but Ieng Sary intervened in the name of Angkar. He opposed the marriage. He said that in Peking you had been one of us and that you do good work."

That is how I came to understand that Angkar had for a long time planned to bring me to Phnom Penh.

"I am flattered," I told him.

As I confided in him more and more, I talked about the things that astonished me. I was struck by the indifference with which young women talked about the evacuation of Phnom Penh: the lost children, the crushed babies, women giving birth along the road, the abandoned and the wounded, the exhausted old people, the crises of hopelessness and suicides . . .

Sikoeun reacted brutally "That's wrong! Everything went very well. Angkar had planned for everything: trucks, clinics, food, and reception at the cooperatives. . . .

We don't have the right to talk like that! Give me the names of those who told you these stories. They are fabricated by the enemy and spread among us by their agents."

"I don't know their names and I don't remember their faces; they all look alike," I said quickly.

I think Sikoeun accepted lies as a matter of form, sensing the uselessness of fighting on this ground and judging that it sufficed to scare me. I swore to myself that I would not share any more confidences.

At the canteen, boys and girls, men and women ate in two distinct groups. Most couples lived separately. Phon's wife lived with Ieng Thirith, and Nane and her son lived in the fenced-in house while Phoeun, the father, settled in a villa.

From the beginning, Angkar stipulated that husbands and wives must live separately. "While the people suffer a thousand ills, and the country is in bad straits, you can't, as members of the vanguard, think of your own happiness. It is good that couples live apart."

The bachelors were given a similar lecture: "Wait until conditions improve. Angkar thinks of you. At the chosen moment, Angkar will marry you."

All of the young combatants had left their families at a very tender age. Boys and girls worked and lived side by side without any problems. They never raised their voices against one another and they did not pick fights.

I liked the combatants. Despite the uniformity of their well-worn black outfits and despite their working the land, they were always well groomed. Each night they showered and washed their clothes—without soap, of course, but everyone and everything was spotless, clean smelling, and of an upright simplicity.

Their days seemed filled with joy. They worked conscientiously and studied seriously. The combatants devoted

48

all of their efforts to serving their people, their country, and the revolution. They asked for nothing in return. "When the economy is straightened out," they said, "we will visit our parents. We will get married when Angkar decides."

An elder from Sikoeun's home area asked me, "Why don't you go visit your mother-in-law? She would love to see she has two beautiful granddaughters!"

Sikoeun had not seen his mother in twenty years, and he had never talked about her. He once told me that, while leaving an underground camp one night for Phnom Penh, he had passed by his village but had not stopped. He was proud of this demonstration of devotion. It showed that he was a real son of Angkar, not shrinking from any sacrifice.

Widowed at a young age, his mother lived alone. She walked with some difficulty due to an illness. At the start of our marriage, I had written her several letters. We heard bits of news saying that her condition was worsening.

I suggested to Sikoeun that we pay his mother a visit. Travel by now was becoming easier, and a cadre from a neighboring village happened to be preparing to set out on a visit to that area. We could have taken advantage of his departure and gone together.

I was excited at the prospect of a trip that might have given me a chance to strengthen my ties to the Khmer community, but Sikoeun objected on the pretext of work, and the trip was put off indefinitely.

Shortly after our arrival in B1, I had noticed sores forming on my daughters' legs and buttocks. They were just mosquito bites, but the heat and humidity had spawned infections, which had spread rapidly. Their bodies, weakened by malnutrition, were unable to respond. I had a moment of panic. Luckily, Ri located an antibiotic powder in the load of medicines waiting to be delivered, and the girls were soon healed. I realized then how vulnerable people in poor countries are to disease.

Next, it was Sikoeun, who suffered a kind of rash on his toes. Again I felt helpless. Not only did I have to combat the disease, I also had to control my reactions to it, being someone who faints at the sight of blood or a wound!

People looked at me suspiciously. "And you, Aunt Phâl, aren't you ill? It must be because the earth accepts you!" I was astonished. To my amusement, they repeated, "The earth accepts you. That's a good sign."

Faced with the need to arm myself against illness, I decided to increase my understanding of acupuncture. I practiced every day to find the sensitive spots. One day, Sikoeun came home from the office seized by a crick in his neck. Not too sure of my science but determined to use it, I plunged several needles into him (after having practiced on myself). Ten minutes later, he left with his head held straight!

The news spread. People came to ask me to relieve stomach pains, lumbago, migraines, and fevers. Every day, I successfully needled one or more patients.

But soon an ominous message was sounded that, bit by bit, grew louder. At first, people simply said, "Do you know that the Angkar doctors are very competent?" or, "Aren't you afraid of causing an accident?" Eventually it was: "Be careful not to undercut the efforts of Angkar doctors!" And finally it became: "Henceforth, all those you touch will incur penalties."

B1 existed, like all of the other units, in a vacuum. The only news we heard from the outside world was brought by new arrivals. One day Ri and I saw two elders arrive from Peking who had rejoined the underground in the next-to-last contingent. We jumped at the chance to ask them about our former comrades.

"All goes well," they said, turning their backs.

But looking at them, we had our doubts. These two students had aged considerably. In one year, Khôn had become hunched up like an old person. Mân, whose svelte bearing and elegance had previously earned her the nickname "Parisian dandy," now had white hair. Their corpselike appearance contradicted their words.

Later we learned that our friends Yaev and Sovong were dead.

"We carried Yaev on a stretcher for five days and five nights before reaching the hospital," Khôn recounted. "But it was already too late. Malaria. . . ."

"Malaria? Is that possible? They had certainly carried quinine and other medicines. . . ."

"Yes, but upon arrival, everything was given to Angkar!"

"And the others?"

"No news. No one knows where they are."

The last Saturday in January, at the assembly point for manual labor, I noticed a lone young woman who looked helpless. She wore blue pants and a blue shirt, and her hair was a bit long compared to revolutionary custom.

"She is Chinese," people said. But Pheap whispered to me, "She is a Cambodian who arrived from Peking."

Little Zheng was born in Cambodia and had left while very young. Her father, now deceased, had been a great leader in the war for independence. Her mother and sisters had returned to Cambodia in 1973. Little Zheng had just arrived and was surprised not to be met by any family members.

"I must see my mother now," she told me. She fidgeted impatiently, stood up, sat back down, crossed one leg over the other.

Hoping to spare her any unpleasant discipline, I warned,

"Crossing legs is a city dweller's habit that is considered reactionary."

She was surprised and seemed not to understand.

"You know," I continued, "the Khmer revolution seeks to be harsher than the Chinese revolution!"

At these words, Little Zheng gave a start. "But that's not possible!" she said.

Little Zheng was baptized *Sar*, which means "message." She was assigned to the team of movers.

The movers' task was to adapt the houses of the wealthy and bourgeois to the revolutionary norm. Only the bare minimum in furniture was to be left—one table, a bed (without a mattress), and a few chairs (without cushions).

The things that could be used by the collectivity—dishes, clothes, and so forth—were sent to a warehouse. Everything else, including tables, furniture, art objects, and books, was thrown out of a window into a truck and later taken to a huge dumping area.

I liked Sar very much. She often visited me and we talked openly. I was like a big sister to her. She played with my daughters and told them Chinese stories. Her visits brought us a breeze of youthful gaiety.

Groping to understand what was happening to her, she tried to establish parallels with China. But Khmer Rouge rigor and discipline had no equivalent. Soon after Sar's arrival, Ri and Pheap left B1. Ri was allowed to join her children, while Pheap went to work at a hospital, which better suited her abilities.

"Ri and Pheap are good influences," people declared pointedly in front of me. "They have a high level of revolutionary conscience. They are worthy of Angkar. That is why Angkar has given them interesting work."

· *Four* ·

An important postwar step had been surmounted with the new rice harvest, but the security problem remained. Under the seal of secrecy, combatants often reported that arrests were taking place and gunshots were erupting night and day in various areas.

Following the evacuation, Phnom Penh was searched from top to bottom to drive out any remaining rebels. Several weeks after the liberation, some were still found in hideouts stocked with provisions. The young ones found it amusing to see that their compatriots, hidden from the sun, had turned white.

All of this, it was hinted, was "the hand of the American imperialists and others plotting to overthrow the new power." It was considered necessary to mount a guard at night.

One night, a loud explosion woke me. A second explosion followed quickly. They were very nearby. Sitting on my bed, holding my breath, I tried to interpret the silence that ensued. To run or to hide? The children rustled on the bed next to me.

"Don't move," their father whispered.

In the atmosphere of terror and death that suddenly enveloped us, each second lasted an eternity. My heart beat so hard, it hurt. I waited, ears alert. We heard noises in the house. My head started to throb. What if we were attacked? Footsteps approached, someone knocked softly at the door.

"Sikoeun, there is a problem. Come!"

Sikoeun left and came back shortly. He led me to the terrace. Several people had already assembled and were looking toward the far side of the garden. Bathed in the strong lights near the hole we had dug to hold well water for the vegetables lay a man stripped to the waist. He had been shot in the leg. Shadowy figures stood around him, but no one seemed to dare to approach him, fearful that he might be hiding a weapon. "We'll have to wait until daybreak to question him," people said.

Commentary bubbled off people's lips. "He threw off his shirt," someone said. "We must find it, it surely holds a message!"

"Maybe he poisoned the water."

"He must have been with someone, since we can't find his shirt!"

"He is awfully fat! The enemy feeds its men well."

"The enemy always sends two men. The other is probably observing us now! Maybe there is a whole gang. We should scout around B1!"

Someone turned brusquely toward me and demanded, "Phâl, go! You must not be seen!"

Shortly after daybreak, the wounded man was still there. He had lost a lot of blood and writhed in a state of semiconsciousness. The spectacle of this young man fighting against death in the middle of a circle of hostile people was unbearable.

Nane took on the responsibility of treating him, while Yaêm, in the name of the Angkar elders, convened a meeting to acclaim "the hero, who by his revolutionary vigilance had struck a terrible blow to the enemy and foiled the plot." The wounded man, now unconscious, was taken to the hospital.

Several days later, I asked Nane what had happened to him. She evaded my question. It was only much later that I learned by chance that the "dreaded enemy" was just a young combatant from the pharmaceutical laboratory next door, a good person who, driven by a malarial fever, had left his room half-dressed. He died.

The mornings were long and the afternoons crept by. In the evening, everyone else went to the assembly, leaving me bored. Bit by bit, the effect of being uprooted had dimmed and the echo of the promising lectures had faded. All that remained was reality: a harder and harder life, divided between the canteen, the garden, and my room. My entire universe was concentrated in a circle of fifty meters where I met the same people, day after day.

Malnutrition sapped my energy. Physical activities and even thoughts were restricted. I was deadened, headed for complete numbness.

Narén and Sokha played and ran around like good children, though their energy levels were lowered, too. The girls wet their beds—a universal signal of emotional disequilibrium.

"Uncles" and "aunts," as all adults were called, according to Khmer custom and tradition, occasionally brought them a "milk apple," a "rose apple," or a *sakeo* —small compensation for displacement. "For the children," they said. I liked how they offered things in a simple and matter-of-fact way.

Among their "uncles," Toun, from the Ministry of Foreign Affairs, sometimes took Narén by bicycle to the kitchens of the guest quarters, where she filled her pockets with candies. I recognized in her my own craving for escape. She resembled me, and people would comment sharply to her about it.

"Sokha is good. She is a good child, she looks like her father. She is Khmer," people could be heard to say. "On the other hand, Narén is French. . . ."

*   *   *

I remained a stranger in the Khmer community. The low-level cadre with whom I worked reported all kinds of unpleasant remarks about me, and Sikoeun was criticized publicly because of me.

"I am always swallowing insults because of you," he complained endlessly.

With time, he found my presence increasingly unbearable. Eventually, weary of the situation and wanting to spare him the reproaches, I took a separate room. There was a small room on the ground floor that nobody wanted because it opened onto the street, making it vulnerable to a commando attack. Less than ten square meters in size, it was a tight fit, but my daughters and I settled in. I found a few pieces of furniture and arranged a charming little corner.

One night, in search of some distraction, under the grill-enclosed house I stumbled upon a quiet gathering. Approaching, I recognized all of the "old guard"—the office workers and the group leaders. They were crouching around a woman who was lecturing. I hid and listened.

"Our revolution is superior to that of the Vietnamese," she said. "The reasons for our success are the evacuation of Phnom Penh, the abolition of money, and the institution of a collective regime."

"Yes, Angkar is brilliant," someone responded. "There are no problems in our country."

"The Vietnamese will never succeed," said another. "Now they would like to imitate us. They send city dwellers to the country, but it is too late."

"They have nothing to eat."

"They don't work."

"They are lazy."

Strong, about forty, her black shirt opened to show a

56

pretty pearled-cotton pullover, the woman seemed happy. She swayed nonchalantly in the middle of her audience. Suddenly she grabbed a baby playing near her with one hand and with the other hand freed her breast to feed the baby.

"Who is that?" I asked the person next to me.

"Shh, quiet! That is Roeun, one of Angkar's highest cadre!"

It was among the elders at B1 that the first contingent of ambassadors was recruited. Tho and Moeun were to go to China, Yôm and Din to Laos, Cheang and Touch to Vietnam, Yaêm and Ni to Korea. All left their children behind, which earned them admiration.

"We have plenty of confidence in Angkar," they declared. "It is our real mother! It is the mother of our children!"

In the meantime, three top political people from the Sihanouk period, Sien An, Duong Som Ol, Sarin Chhak, and their wives, along with Toch Kam Doeun and Vanna, were recalled to B1 after serving satisfactorily for a brief period at the base.

The departure of the new contingent of ambassadors coincided with the recall of ambassadors from the previous period. They were assembled in a place kept secret except from Moch, the wife of the secretary to the embassy in Peking, who came to B1. She had a six year old and a six month old and was expecting a third child. Her mother, a descendant of the Sisowath family, had joined the underground at the beginning of the war.

Many people grumbled about having someone of royal blood at B1. "The cadres of the moment" were eager for their revenge. They laughed with scorn at the outcome reserved for the former diplomats.

57

"They led the sweet life while we slept under the sky. They should suffer now!"

"They gorged on fine foods while we were hungry. The sides have changed now!"

"They don't know how to hold a hoe or drive in a nail. They're amusing themselves! They'll learn!"

Moch was housed in the first floor of a villa looking out upon Granny-cakes's courtyard. Like everywhere else, furnishings were sparse. Moch complained of the material conditions. She openly protested against the food, which she deemed inadequate for her children and unsuitable for her, given her condition. Then she called for a car to go for rides . . . In a word, she lost her footing in the immensity of the upheavals in her daily life.

Madame Duong, with her inexhaustible patience and sweet wisdom, tried to make Moch accept the reality at hand, but she remained numb to the woman's advice. One day she went to the house where her marriage had been celebrated. Searching through the remains of successive pillages, she solemnly retrieved a little silk purse, which she took back with her.

Moch readily spoke of the splendors of bygone days, which only deepened her isolation among those who considered her an enemy of the people. Vanna and I often went to talk with her, but Moch writhed about in her own distress and would not accept the hand we were extending to her. One day she wrote the government, begging to be allowed to leave—in vain, of course. Seeing no hope, she threatened to throw herself out of the window. People only laughed at her.

Moch buried herself inexorably in her misery, while we, unable to do anything and afraid of being accused of complacency or complicity, gave up.

*　　*　　*

The election of the first people's assembly was held at the end of March 1976. It did not generate much interest. With the condition that Cambodia was in, one must question the conditions under which the voting took place.

Shortly thereafter, Prince Sihanouk's retirement as head of state and the composition of the new government were simultaneously announced. Smelling power firmly in their hands, the elders were jubilant. Khieu Samphan was pushed aside and Pol Pot, who was then an unknown, took over as prime minister.

In early April, a new, three-cycle seminar was organized to correspond to the different participants' ideological levels. I was excluded from all three, which alarmed me. The time of seminars often marked a renewal of ideological tension, and I could sense the hostility building up around me.

"Among us are spies in the pay of the CIA and of France," I heard all around me. Such ideas, no doubt directed at me, should have made me laugh. Instead, in a state of physical and moral fatigue, I took them very seriously.

Wherever I was assigned, I kept my children close to me. They always found something to do, were undemanding, and never fought between themselves. One day I found a doll for them and dressed it in black. They jumped with joy. They played with it inside for a moment and then took it out for a walk. I watched them as they left. I was touched to see them both so sweet and gentle, despite all of our privations and difficulties.

My daughters' sudden screams jarred me from my work. Roeun had seized the doll and was waving it above the children, whose desperate attempts to recover the toy were in vain.

"Do you see this?" Roeun scolded. "They are amusing themselves with puppets now! Have you ever seen peasants playing with puppets?" And all of Roeun's followers abjectly made fun of the girls.

From that day on, I was harassed about my children. I was accused of being a mother hen and of educating my daughters along bourgeois and capitalist principles.

"Children are a blank page on which we can write anything we want," the old guard said, plagiarizing Mao. "When they get a revolutionary education, they become revolutionaries. But you, you imprint French concepts on their character. You're making them bourgeois with imperialist and revisionist ideas. You are doing them a great wrong!"

Finally, they asked me to give the children to Li during the day. I gladly accepted. Li handled Din and Moeun's children intelligently. I had often hoped that she could similarly accept mine. But until now, people had responded that "we should not mix the dish towels and the table napkins."

I took them to Li's.

"See you tonight," I said. "Enjoy yourselves!"

That night, Roeun's followers came to announce that my girls were content with Li and would like to spend the night there.

The next day, I went to visit them. All morning I had been going around in circles, like a cat that has lost her kittens. I found them eating a grapefruit.

"Children have a special diet," Li told me. "Angkar gives them bread, fruit, sugar, candy, cakes. Angkar thinks of their health, since the country's future depends on them."

Narén and Sokha, seated with the other children, were savoring their first fruit in a long time. They bit delicately into the flesh and, with a kind of contemplative reverence, kept the pulp in their mouths as long as possible. Staring into the center of the circle, they acted as if they didn't see me.

I turned away sadly, thinking that Angkar had found a powerful tool—food—to keep my children from me. At that point, Roeun approached me. "Aunt Phâl," she said, "you should not visit your daughters continually. It upsets Angkar! When they don't see you, they don't cry. They are happier with Angkar, you should be sure of that."

Once the seminar was over, the leaders, newly invigorated, conscious of their responsibilities, and worried about improving their efficiency, reorganized the entire unit. That is how the children's community came to be moved to a villa across the street from my room. So, while obeying the rules and having the girls only on rare visits, I at least had the joy of seeing them and hearing them play.

The group of young boys and girls soon numbered more than ten. Li took care of them with much dedication— one never heard any shouting, crying, or fighting. An extraordinary sense of solidarity reigned among them.

Li took care of everything: the washing up, the bathroom, and the drive to the canteen. When it was time to shower, the children undressed, put their dirty garments to one side, chose and arranged their change of clothes, and then passed in single file in front of Li, who soaped them down with precise, rapid motions. The children raised their arms, exposed one ear after the other, and finally crouched so that Li, with one swift gesture, could wipe their bottoms clean. Coming out of the tub-shower, the children enveloped themselves in a *krâmar*—a shawl—and smiled, revealing their small, white milk teeth, happy to be clean and fresh and smelling good.

One day at noon, Narén came to me, sat down, and

took my arm and caressed it. I was moved by this tender gesture. I wanted to hold her in my arms when she suddenly asked me, "Why do you have white skin? Why is your nose pointed?"

I gave a start, and she continued, "Why aren't you like the others?" Then she left running.

For six months I had been living in Phnom Penh and asking myself what Angkar's intentions toward me were. I had the feeling of being a symbol with many uses: I could be the incarnation of capitalism and imperialism or, on the contrary, the spitting image of the internationalist heroine, ready to make any sacrifice for the revolution. And now?

One day, I asked Sikoeun, "Since political life is beginning anew, with diplomats settling in Phnom Penh and international opinion interested in Cambodia's fate, why not put out an information bulletin in foreign languages?"

As he hesitated, I continued: "It would be enough to reprint and translate certain news items broadcast every day toward the country's interior. . . ."

He tried to discourage me, but I insisted. He ended up agreeing to my suggestion while imposing certain conditions.

Starting the next day, I recorded the morning broadcast and translated it. At lunch, I gave the papers to Sikoeun. I continued to do this every day.

On April 17, the first anniversary of the liberation, I listened to the long speech read by Khieu Samphan and then undertook to translate it. This work gave me great pleasure. But to my surprise, when I gave the paper to Sikoeun, he became angry. "This is not your work," he told me. "You can't translate such a serious document!" The translation ended up in the wastebasket.

62

*　　*　　*

Three months after announcing that we were entering an era of prosperity, Angkar brought us sacks of rice with English and Chinese words on them. We'd had rice the first few days after the harvest, but bouillon at noon and soup at night had soon become the norm again.

This rice was so old that people in the West would certainly have refused to eat it, but of course there was never any question of lodging complaints. Several girls were put to work sorting it.

While separating the rice, we became covered with its white powder. Work stopped fifteen minutes before the meal so that we could change clothes. No one ever showed up for a meal in a sloppy or dirty outfit.

That same day, as I was getting ready to return to my room and change, I saw a column of people I did not recognize on the path we were obliged to take. I carefully observed the arrival of these strangers and was surprised to see Chau Séng, followed by former diplomats and high functionaries.

I'd heard that Chau Séng had the habit of showing a certain flexibility in order "to climb the sugar palm," one of the Cambodian peasantry's most dangerous tasks. By that he hoped to prove that he had remained loyal to his ideal of social progress.

He stopped. A naturally friendly man, he started talking. "My standard of living has dropped miserably," he said. "But I must say I don't lack for anything essential. I have learned a lot and am happy to report that in certain areas and certain places, there is considerable progress. . . ."

With the month of May came mango season. "Phnom Penh is overflowing with them," reported the workers who moved household furnishings from place to place—the only people authorized to leave camp B1 and navigate about town. They used their leisure time to gather mangoes. They brought them back by the carload. Between the "four seasons" mango, with its clear flesh, and the "elephant's head," red but tasteless, there were many varieties. Without contest, the best was the *kti*, medium-sized and elongated, fine and slightly curved, like the body of a siren.

We ate all we could consume. In just a few days, one could see the faces getting rounder and taking on color. The mangoes did us all a lot of good.

There was such an abundance of fruit that Madame Duong suggested making preserves. The idea was reluctantly approved by the cooks, who feared it would impinge upon the conception of revolutionary cooking.

Preparing and cooking the preserves was a tedious and difficult task. Sar and I helped out.

"The preserves will be better," Madame Duong suggested, "if we add a bit of coconut milk."

This would have meant picking a coconut—just one—and the cooks opposed it. "What more do you want?" they asked us. "You are given the little finger and you demand the whole arm!"

Madame Duong did not insist, and the process continued. It lasted several days. She spread the preserve paste out in the sun on smooth plates. There was so much of it that we envisioned treating everybody in B1. Completing this task proved to be a real joy.

Once the drying was complete, Madame Duong was sad to discover that her delicacies soon disappeared. She complained to the head cook, who shrugged his shoulders. "That is what happens when you deviate from Angkar's line!" he replied.

Sey arrived alone one morning at B1. Everyone was surprised, but no one asked where she had been. Sey had a round face, clear skin, pretty little white teeth, amber-colored eyes, and little arched eyebrows, and her hair was as fine as silk thread. Sey was Saom's fiancée. She came to join him for their wedding.

The austere ceremony was simultaneously organized late one night for several couples around an empty table placed in front of a red flag. It was held after a long day of work, like all of the others, and before another day's work, just like the others.

Once married, Sey and Saom behaved like complete strangers in public. They worked in their assigned areas, one in the office and the other in the garden. Sey bubbled with activity and joie de vivre. In the canteen, he ate with the men, she with the women. The young couple's modesty seemed only to add grace to their love.

Sey told me how her parents, her father a doctor and her mother a nurse, had joined the underground when they were very young. She said the unit to which she had been assigned was in charge of guiding a group of children who had arrived from Peking in 1973. Among them was Saom.

Camp B17 was one of the most difficult. Food was extremely scarce. The work—and test—of the group of students was to put into use a piece of land totally unfit for cultivation.

After the liberation, Saom and his friend Roeth were assigned to the Ministry of Foreign Affairs. No news was ever heard of the others from the camp.

Sey found herself in a textile factory, where she learned to weave and to dye fabrics. Sey spoke enthusiastically about her work. She explained how she and her companions had organized themselves to keep the machines going night and day. Their biggest problem was a lack of basic materials.

Sey's weaver's eye noticed that my dress fitted poorly. I was wearing a sarong dyed with huge flowers, and the floral patterns stood out boldly. It was undeniably ugly. "I could dye some cloth for a *sampot*," she proposed.

65

"That is very kind, but I have come with empty hands!"

"It would suffice to find a curtain."

"A curtain?"

It dawned on me what she had in mind, and I searched through various houses. The only curtain I could find was hanging in the window of my husband's room.

Three days later, I was wearing a magnificent *sampot*, jet black, long, and as full as one could wish.

Sey talked about her life in the underground with pride, intelligence, and simplicity. I listened to her with great admiration. She recounted the evacuation of Phnom Penh: "The army entered Phnom Penh at nine. White flags were everywhere. The population was in the streets applauding. Everyone was happy. Suddenly, gunfire broke out, very close to here, toward the market. The order was given to chase everyone out within forty-eight hours . . . the sick, children, wounded, aged, pregnant, everyone was expelled—by force of arms."

It was the first time that I had heard an opinion different than that of Angkar on this recent history. She continued: "Phnom Penh was evacuated by force, and the co-ops weren't ready to accommodate the new arrivals. To feed and house the evacuated, they had neither food nor lodging. . . ."

Since the night she had come to give us her account of events seated on the bench outside, Roeun the Feudal, as I nicknamed her, came more and more often to camp B1. After a few visits as observer, she took to criticizing and giving orders.

Roeun became Ieng Sary's right hand. Feeling her new-found power, she installed people from her clan as team leaders. One day she did a favor for her niece Voeun by giving her a car and chauffeur to visit Taing Kauk, a village in Kampong Thom Province, where her mother lived.

After returning, Voeun was never the same. This young woman, with her child's face ringed by curly hair, had lost her cheer and playfulness. Her face now solemn, Voeun was silent for several days. Eventually she recounted her traumatic experience: "In the countryside, the hospitals are full. Sick people are being refused. They sleep on the floor. In Taing Kauk, twenty to thirty die every day; whole families are thrown in a common grave. . . ."

I looked at her. There was no doubt that she was telling the truth. Others turned away and continued their work.

At the beginning of June, Angkar sent a truck of corn. "As members of a revolutionary unit," Roeun told us, "we must perform our tasks, provide for ourselves, and provide a surplus for the state. The cooperatives have a heavy burden—we can't depend on them. In fact, we need from now on to give them aid. Angkar has sent us this truckload of maize, and you will shell it for the next sowings."

When the first load of maize was shelled, a second came—then a third and a fourth. We spent all of our evenings shelling maize by hand. Young combatants, usually cheery while doing manual labor, hardly dared to talk in front of those who worked in the offices and were themselves guarded in starting conversation. The atmosphere was very sad.

The undertaking continued. We were on perhaps the tenth truckload when Roeun came to congratulate us on our "high revolutionary consciousness." "The cooperatives work a lot," she added. "Between now and the next harvest are six long months of painful work for our brother and sister peasants."

"Here, we have no needs," responded a team leader who had been preselected to "launch the masses." "We understand Angkar's concern and we are wholeheartedly with the people. We now have rice soup at two meals. That is a lot when you think that elsewhere the ration is reduced. We could mix this rice and send the surplus to Angkar. We are determined to agree to all sacrifices."

"We are determined to agree to all sacrifices," the group repeated in unison.

It was our turn. Once again we saw the shelled maize replace the rice in our daily soup. The maize was too old and had to be cooked with lime, and still it was indigestible! Nevertheless, no one complained. Each remained convinced, as the propaganda affirmed, that the situation in the countryside was generally good and that the next harvest would go down in history.

· Five ·

The rainy season advanced, but nature remained deeply scarred by the drought. Only the throbbing croak of the buffalo toad convinced us of the monsoon's arrival.

Moch gave birth alone one night after dinner. Having taken her pulse using the Chinese method, I knew she was expecting a boy. I hoped I was wrong, she so wanted a girl. But it was in fact a boy, a magnificent baby. Nature is unpredictable! How could such a beautiful baby be born from this weak, depressed, undernourished woman?

Moch, who had undergone a cesarean section for the birth of her first child and been in intensive care for the second, preferred to give birth alone this time. She must have been very frightened of the revolutionary doctors.

We could guess the nightmare she must have lived through during the long months of waiting. Now, the one link that had kept her going, the hope of a girl, disappeared, and she let herself go. She lay flat out, pale as death, without moving, at the edge of the abyss. She did not hear the child crying near her and did not see those who came to visit.

She was encouraged to breast-feed the baby. "I didn't have milk for the other two," she replied. "How could I have any for this one?"

"Sorya, Sihanouk's daughter, who is more of a princess than you, didn't have milk either. Now she does."

"I don't have any milk," Moch repeated.

"Angkar gives special rations to those who give birth. We're going to prepare caramelized pork hocks and chicken giblets. In return, do what you need to do to have milk!"

Moch extended her breast to her strong baby, but in vain. Angkar finally offered a diet of concentrated milk, albeit not without adding, "Milk is reserved for the very sick. In the former society, when people of your class were in power, people were left out in the cold! Don't ever forget Angkar's generosity."

Born with a veritable *force de nature*, the baby grew quickly and soon showed tender smiles and gurgled charmingly. But Moch was out of reach; she did not respond to his smiles or show interest in his development. She carried the child about without any feeling of pleasure and seemed to hardly see him.

In the middle of the season, manpower at camp B1 increased by 150 people, divided between the team of movers (the most important), various manual labor teams, and office personnel, which never exceeded a dozen.

The "uncles" and "aunts" at the offices decided to extend their manual labor area. From one day to the next, they had the habit of descending in a group at exactly 4:00 P.M. and making off with the watering cans and all of the yokes used by the manual labor team to carry them. Then they would lift their pantlegs, roll up their sleeves, and put themselves to work with great fervor.

Sarin Chhak and Duong Som Ol, despite their age, were particularly noticeable in how energetically they threw themselves into their work. Sarin Chhak made no fewer than fifty round-trips from the bottom of the water hole to the little planting bed.

To those among the combatants who asked themselves if it was reasonable for a man that age to exert himself so, Roeun grumbled, "Peasants, they do up to one hundred trips, with even heavier loads. . . ."

Duong Som Ol devoted himself to making watering cans. With tin cans, pieces of corrugated iron, and chunks of wood, he managed to make magnificent watering cans. His was solid, quality work that everyone admired. Both he and Sarin Chhak had been part of the former elite and had known its honors and privileges. People were pleased to see that they had been able to manage such a remarkable change.

As for myself, I found a simple satisfaction and happiness in the manual work and community life. I detached myself from what heretofore had been the daily routine. I discovered a new sensitivity in myself and learned a new way of loving. I was surprised that I was doing so well. I had access to an inner life that was becoming richer and I was content with my daughters' development and progress. What was more, my papers began to be appreciated.

"The great Ieng Sary declared in front of everybody that he hadn't found one translation error in your last work," Ane, a colleague, announced joyfully one evening.

Moments later, Sikoeun brought confirmation. Triumphantly, he said, "You see? I told you so! Angkar is taking care of you. It never fails. One day, when you have made progress, it will reward you."

One night, Sikoeun announced that he was joining a delegation going to Sri Lanka the next day. I was thrilled. "You'll be able to send my mother a note to tell her everything is going fine," I said.

"If Angkar suggests it," he responded. "But there are security problems. . . ." Seeing my astonishment, he continued: "You, you are controlled, but your mother is not controlled! International plots exist that seek to eliminate Angkar and the elders, you understand?"

I understood nothing of their paranoia, but I did understand that he was not going to do as I asked.

"Regarding the bulletins, you should continue as usual," he said. "Give them to Mi, Ieng Sary's secretary. He'll correct them."

On the first day of Sikoeun's absence, after finishing the translations, I took them to Mi, who received them without saying a word. The next day, I brought the new papers and took back the ones from the preceding day, which were supposed to be distributed in the early afternoon. Mi told me he had not had time to look at them.

Several days passed in this manner. Refusing to let it deter me, I brought my papers in each morning and took back those from the day before. But my efforts were in vain. Mi made it clear that he was too busy to correct them.

Finally, judging that the game had lasted long enough, I walked into Mi's office one morning. Mân was at the typewriter, pecking laboriously with two fingers.

"You want your papers?" Mi asked. "Mân is in the process of typing them."

"I could help you," I said. "What takes you hours, I can do quickly."

"The important thing is not to go fast or slow. The important thing is the political viewpoint of the person translating. I taped the broadcasts and compared them with your translations. You don't translate word for word!"

"That's right, I summarize."

"That is exactly where the problem lies."

"You know perfectly well that these articles can't be literally translated. It would be indecipherable."

"Each word is important. You only make them up in

your head. You and Sikoeun, you do whatever comes to mind—it's organized sabotage. . . ."

Mi went on and on. I left his office deeply shaken. Lost in my thoughts, I was walking like an automaton. Near the kitchen, the truck loaded with garbage was about to take off for Stung Mean Chey.

To hell with their manias! Going for a ride will do me good! I said to myself. I quickly wrapped my *krâmar* around my face and put a foot on the wheel hub. With one bound, I straddled the rails and landed in the garbage. I was going to take a little tour of Phnom Penh, my first sortie since coming to Camp B1.

The town had been cleaned, but the houses were still abandoned. At Stung Mean Chey, the truck turned over; we had a terrible time putting it back on its wheels.

Back at B1, I found myself eye to eye with Mân, who was looking for me. He acted very serious and suspicious. I didn't much care. My little escape had changed my ideas.

"We need a paper that had been given to you to type," he said. "There were some corrections that you did not take into account."

"It must be in the wastebasket," I said.

"We searched, but found nothing."

"You conduct searches in people's absence!" I exclaimed, astonished by my own audacity, then set out in search of the missing document.

I was informed that Sokha was sick. With a bound, I started for the children's home, where I found my daughter stretched out, limp. I leaned over her and took her tiny hands. Her stare, desperately empty, was fixed on the roof.

"She has had a fever for several days," Nane told me. "We have given her shots, but her temperature does not go down."

I was frightened and immediately forgot my other worries. During her first seventy months, my daughter had survived one fever after another, her breathing resembling a little flame in the wind. All of my past anxieties came back to me. I decided to stay near her. I took her little feet in my hands and pressed with my fingertips on the insides of her big toes, at the spot called *Rong* in acupuncture. I did the same for the *Quchi* point at the folds of her elbows. The sleeping child let herself be handled. By midnight, her temperature had gone down. She took a little water and dozed off. I continued to massage until dawn, then dozed off.

In the morning, I went back to see Sokha. She was in the courtyard, among her friends. She was not very strong, but the flame of life once again shone in her eyes.

For me, there could be no greater joy.

In the days that followed my confrontation with Mi, I continued to pass on my translations to him before willingly joining the manual work team of which I enjoyed being a part.

Mi and Mân left me in peace. But as the days passed, I could not help thinking about the fateful date of Si-koeun's return. He would not miss the opportunity to reproach me and demand explanations.

One night, they came to fetch me. I was being called to the "leader." "They are showing a film made in the region of Battambang," they explained en route. "The leader wants to take it along for the closing of the Sri Lanka conference. We need to record accompanying text in English."

The movie, filmed in eight millimeter, showed village scenes, plantings using tractors, and planted rice fields. Although technically mediocre, its defects gave it an air of authenticity that was lacking in Chinese documentaries.

All morning, I practiced reading the text. The recording

went well. The operator, an experienced technician, was very pleased. "Among the young ones who come to the radio station, some can barely read," he told me. "People have to whisper words to them and make them learn the text by heart. To record ten minutes' worth, it takes a half-day of work. . . ."

When Sikoeun returned from the conference, I innocently asked him what he thought of the movie.

"What movie?" he asked. When I explained, he became angry. "I can't turn my back for a minute without you doing stupid things! What does that show? Here, it's different from abroad. You are under Angkar's responsibility! A Cambodian woman understands that, but you, you are too imbued with your personality! That's French education for you, imperialist education!"

As Sikoeun carried on his diatribe, I admitted to myself that I was not proud to be reduced to living passively in the shadow of a husband who shunned me and was afraid of me.

"Modesty is something you don't know about!" he continued. "You never yield. You don't know how to submit. Why? Because you feel you are owner of your own personality! Individuality! The uniqueness of your personality, that is the principal enemy!" Then he stormed away.

Roeun surveyed the scene from morning till night and did not haggle over recommendations and directives. Her principal preoccupation was to steer the unit toward self-sufficiency. That is how she came to organize a project to put into cultivation all of the land within the perimeter of the unit. Each team was allotted a section. I participated in the clearing of an area planted with banana trees where a little wooden house stood. "That must have been where the guards lived," the young people said.

The interior of the hut was a spectacle: beds and tables

turned over, pillows ripped, mats torn, broken charcoal burners tossed pell-mell between a shattered cupboard and a sideboard. Orders were given to break down the walls and remove the roof tiles. "Those who lived here have no further need of this hut," commented the team leader.

In the wink of an eye, everything was cleared away and we were already raking the ground when we heard the plow strike something metallic. "Everyone hit the ground!" someone commanded. Unearthing mines was common and often caused serious accidents.

The alert passed and we uncovered the object. It was a munitions box filled with photos, children's clothes, and identity papers. As the contents of the box were displayed, we were able to reconstitute the lives of those who had occupied the house: a young couple, two children, and an old woman. He had been an enlisted soldier under Lon Nol. Their whole fortune was displayed in front of us. "They were enemies!" declared the team leader. "If they have hidden themselves, we'll find them one day or another. . . ."

As the cottage had been dismantled, so were the banana trees uprooted—as if, by the time it took to say which would go, there was no longer any use for them.

The second theme of Roeun's proposal was to reinforce collectivism and divide the groups into teams. Members of each team were supposed to remain together—working, taking meals, and resting together. Under no conditions were the teams to mix.

Roeun thus ordered anew the rearrangement of occupants of the various locations, which is how Sikoeun and I found ourselves sharing a small, isolated villa with Toch and Vanna. This separation, which demonstrated the fierce demarcation between old and new, did not augur well. Sikoeun used it as an excuse to speak out angrily.

"I have suffered a thousand ills since joining the resistance," he declared. "You saw the skeletal state I found myself in? I withstood all that to be worthy of my country and my people. By now, I should be with the elders. But because of you, I am with the newcomers. Because of you, all of the sacrifices I have consented to, all of the sufferings I endured, count for nothing!"

A few days later, as I was going to the usual assembly point, Choeun, the new team leader, approached me. "Aunt Phâl, why don't you rest today!" he said. "The instructions have already been issued. The team is at work. Angkar has nothing slated for you."

It was the same for the following days, and so I was gently excluded from the manual labor team.

Every morning, I continued to do my translations. Eventually I was invited to come to the offices in the evening, after the end of the work day, to assist in correcting my work.

Sikoeun became more aggressive every day, and the correcting sessions lasted longer and longer into the night. For this task, Sikoeun was joined by Mân. The two of them quibbled for hours over my choice of phrases.

"You must translate word for word," they told me. "Each word is important. You just do it in your head. You translate in spite of your good sense. You deliberately sabotage. You are harder than rock!"

Back in my room, I typed the stencils so that they could be printed and distributed the next morning.

"Don't you think we could organize the work in a more rational way?" I suggested to Sikoeun one day.

"Rational to you!" he responded. "You only think about yourself! There you go with your Western logic, but what Angkar decides is always well founded."

An anonymous, faceless power, Angkar was omnipresent, blindly followed and idolized. Angkar demanded to be served unconditionally, and in return, it provided everything. Angkar banished all religions and beliefs, imposing itself like a new god.

Its impact on the young combatants was considerable. They adopted it without thinking or discussing all of the "teachings." It was taken for granted that the most beautiful and most heroic of all the peoples on the earth were the people of Cambodia. Nothing and no one could equal them. The Vietnamese were hypocritical and lazy, the Thais were loafers and gamblers, the Lao were too few to warrant an epithet. Whites were devils and blacks were vulgar savages.

Isolation and division reinforced Angkar's ideological control. Added to this was the fact that each person was constantly tormented by hunger. Angkar played on this with great finesse.

Everyone wanted to become Angkar's ideal proletarian, motivated *by* Angkar and *for* Angkar.

While the ideological work was becoming radicalized, the food was getting worse. Roeun assigned one of her cousins, Sean, to be head cook. She was an experienced woman, but there was no longer anything to put into the pot. More and more often, we ate maize two meals a day.

"Soon Angkar will bake bread for you," Roeun said. "In the cooperatives, the harvest is about to begin. We in Phnom Penh have no needs. In a short while, all will go well."

The children's situation became a cause for concern. Roeun had replaced Li with two of her nieces. They were horrible people. From the child center we often heard screams and crying.

"There is nothing to be gotten from Narén and Sokha," I heard. "They don't want to learn anything; their heads are harder than rock," or else, "Sokha has done her self-criticism. She will not wet her bed anymore. She has decided not to eat the peasants' rice for three days."

My daughters' heads were shaved, leaving them unrecognizable and hideous-looking. Their small, thin bodies were covered with abscesses. "They ate too much sugar as babies," I was told.

They watched me when I walked in front of the courtyard, their big black eyes reflecting infinite sadness. But, held back by fear, they did not approach me.

I spoke to Sikoeun about what was in store for the girls, and he answered, "You don't know what you're talking about. You repeat anything. With Angkar, the children are treated well. You can't be hearing your children cry, you can't!" I insisted, and he raised his voice. "Let me tell you one thing: you are either for the revolution or you are against it. In Cambodia, we don't compromise. What Angkar does is good and fair. Your daughters don't need you. Angkar looks after their Khmer education. You must be convinced of it. You don't take into account all of the damage you caused in their first years of life!"

Sunk in his chair, he looked me up and down with the expression of the grand inquisitor and concluded, "Everything leads me to believe that you don't sincerely support our revolution. Consciously or not, you oppose it! You sabotage it!"

Stunned, I withdrew silently. Once alone, I questioned myself. Was Sikoeun right? Was I being led by unknown forces commanding me to act against interests I thought I wanted to defend? Shaken to the core, I balanced on the edge of ruin. Tears of hopelessness welled up within me. I tried to get a hold of myself. "Don't cry, don't cry!" a voice within me said.

Then I recalled what my mother had often said to me when I was little: "I said 'life is mean,' the echo said 'sing.' " I started singing. I made up the words. I called out for freedom. And I cried while singing my heart out.

*　　*　　*

Several days passed, but I could not continue. I knew that if I didn't find a way out of this unbearable situation, I would risk sinking into madness. The time to dream was over; I needed to put an end to the experiment I had hoped to see come to fruition. But how to escape from this trap? Take flight? Impossible—Phnom Penh was itself a prison. One couldn't leave one's unit without immediately being spotted and taken away by Security.

I decided to talk to Sikoeun. "I can't waste more of my time," I declared. "I offered my services unselfishly but, after a year, still have nothing to do. I consider that the contract is broken. I want to leave."

"I will submit your request to Angkar," he answered, scarcely concealing his enthusiasm.

Three days later, he gave me the decision: I could leave, but the children had to stay!

I jumped at this edict. Sikoeun flashed me a look that was sharper than any blade. He studied my reaction.

If I insist, I thought to myself, he will have me done away with. The girls will be beaten and starved and we will each die in our own way. Short of dying, I prefer that we stay together.

So I turned in upon myself. I developed what I called two-sided armor. I refused to allow any feelings or thoughts to show. At the same time, I protected myself from any outside influences and psychological pressures. I hoped to pull myself out of it, but I knew the battle would be hard.

At the end of September, a new series of seminars was organized. Roeun, in whom Ieng Sary had vested all powers, was designated to preside over the studies. The session opening was marked by a thundering broadcast of "The International" along the width of the big, open windows:

Arise, ye prisoners of starvation
Arise, ye wretched of the earth
For justice thunders condemnation
A better world's in birth. . . .

The wing I had been assigned to was isolated from everybody and everything. During the day, I could have been whisked away and no one would have known. If I had been attacked, no one would have heard my screams. In the face of constant danger, I felt an indescribable fear.

Excluded from the seminars as well as from the manual labor, and unable to stay in my room doing nothing, I began to do some cleaning and weeding. And, since I could neither leave nor escape, I devoted myself to raising vegetables. The only available space was the old stone walkway in front of my residence—if only it would hold out, I would get the dirt.

I took some planks from the pigpen and dug some long ditches, then went as far afield as five hundred meters looking for soil. Plank after plank, patiently, obstinately, I filled the rows. The work, which no one asked me to do, gave me a sense of freedom. I felt a new strength and relative peace.

After filling the first four rows, Sean suggested I plant *khanna* cabbage, which is coveted for its taste, especially when sautéed. They would likely be sent to the diplomatic store as evidence of support for Angkar. I accepted mainly out of curiosity—and not without realizing it was a gamble. I was careful and the plants were growing, when one morning, to my horror, I discovered that some chickens and their chicks had nibbled the buds of the plants. My crop was in jeopardy.

Hong, who was there, smiled and said, "It doesn't matter, Aunt Phâl, we'll take care of it!" That same afternoon, four young fellows from the office workers' vegetable garden appeared with stakes, wire, netting, axes, and pliers, and in no time at all, they had built a wall more than two meters high between my area and the rest of the unit.

"You intrigue me," Sar said. "You are put in quarantine, you don't talk to anyone, but you see everything, nothing escapes you. People would say you penetrate people to read their thoughts!"

There was some truth in what she said. From the self-control of words to the self-control of thought, I had come to see myself thinking and acting like a stranger. It gave me a strange power over myself and others. I dominated the situation. I could ascertain motives, I foresaw effects, and I controlled reactions in a very instinctive way.

I immediately noticed changes in mood and attitude, which allowed me to analyze what was happening. Unable to communicate in the language of the Revolution, I felt all kinds of vibrations. Some people gave off an aura of gentleness, others seemed icy or inspired revulsion. I saw people through a kind of halo, luminous or pale, frankly, very somber indeed.

In November, when the corn was used up, minced bindweed was added to the soup water. While cooking, the bindweed secreted a black juice that was plentiful but unappetizing.

Sean, good cook that she was, made soups from next to nothing—herbs, banana tree trunk, stumps. Some days she didn't have a single thing to put in the pot.

She complained one day that she couldn't do her job. "Angkar," she said, "should be able to feed us a little better." The next day, she received a basket of spoiled eggs and a basket of fruit, also rotten. We still ate them . . .

*   *   *

With the return of the dry season, the garden teams doubled their efforts. I wanted to produce the finest vegetables, too. Knowing nothing about gardening, I watched and imitated. Then I tried out a few ideas of my own. I especially wanted to experiment with the influence of deprivation on green cabbage plants. One morning, I aerated the soil and left the plants dry. By sunset, they were so weak that their little leaves tossed about in the breeze. When the sun went down, I carefully gave them a dose of manure. The next day, I watered them copiously. The effect was astonishing! The plants seemed to straighten up before my very eyes. From one day to the next, I saw them fill out and spread across the ground. They were magnificent. Roeun quickly ordered a car to pick up the harvest, which she reserved for the foreigners. The average weight per cabbage was one and one-half kilos. I was satisfied with my achievement, of course, but it also reminded me that hunger is a terribly efficient weapon.

During the December indoctrination course, the atmosphere became heavy and the translation correction meetings more frenzied. On top of problems of style were the political ones. Everything was political; each word was closely examined. Sikoeun and Mân took turns criticizing my work: "Why did you not translate under the righteous direction of the revolutionary Organization, conforming to the original?"

"Because it was already written two lines before and two lines farther along. . . ."

"Do you imagine that 'under the righteous direction of the revolutionary Organization' is ever written too often? Its direction is righteous; it must be said and repeated with pride! And to say it, one must be convinced. In your way of thinking, we can see that you are scornful of it and that your real motivation is to sabotage the work!"

Subjected for so long to highly deficient foods and hard work, I had lost almost twenty-five pounds in less than six months! The inevitable happened: I developed an edema—excessive swelling of the legs.

Sikoeun, capitalizing on my weakness, judged the moment right to push me even further. "While we are at the office, we don't know what you do alone here," he said one night. "You could well be contacting spy rings. . . ." Then he slapped me and tweaked my nose. "It is people with a pointed nose, like you, who plundered our country and murdered our people!" he concluded.

Having failed with force, he tried to evoke compassion. Stretching out on the bed, mouth open as if in agony, he said he had stomach cancer. "We can't both be sick," he moaned. "Imagine the cost to Angkar!"— even though despite my weakness, I had not stopped working. I had continued to translate, type, and water my vegetables.

As the tension mounted throughout the evening, Sikoeun declared, "You don't understand anything about the socialist revolution!"

"That is possible," I answered. "That which I see around me is so edifying!"

Without picking up on the irony in my voice, he continued: "You never got beyond the national democratic revolution. . . ."

"Ah, yes?" I said, stunned. "Where did that come from?"

Then I let myself go: "First, know that being French, I lived the democratic revolution two hundred years ago! Second, the country that I come from has never needed a national revolution. And third, in matters of revolution, France has nothing to learn from Kampuchea!"

He said nothing for once; perhaps he was not listening.

The dry season brought spring temperatures and, with the heat, the maturation of the rice crop—which is why Angkar chose this time to invite and receive foreign delegations. Toward mid-December, Sikoeun accompanied a Lao delegation. The first morning after his departure, as I prepared to protect my new cabbage plantation from the sun, I encountered Ane and Vanna. "You must have a lot of work," they said. "We have come to help you."

After months of being surrounded by hostility, however, this friendly act seemed abnormal. Their conduct scared me; I wondered about their hidden intentions. "You know very well that I work alone every day," I responded coldly. They left without a word, leaving me distressed that I had not been able to renew my friendships with these two women.

The next day, as I was leaving the canteen, Roeun approached me. She invited me to the children's house and brought along a package. Then she sat on the stairs and began talking. "Angkar is taking care of you at the highest level," she told me, patting her hand on my back. I winced. "You work too much, far too much!" she continued. "You only have skin left on your bones! Angkar doesn't want that. . . . Yesterday, during a high-level meeting, and I mean the highest level, we talked about you. Angkar is pleased with you and will soon prove it. You'll see. . . . In waiting, regain your strength and take this." And she handed me the package.

"Tomorrow, I'll send you something else. Now rest! Don't forget that Angkar cares about everyone's health, and especially yours. . . ."

The bread Roeun gave me smelled good. It smelled so good that the fragrance filled my every pore and caused a sweet sensation inside me.

Crossing the fence that separated me from the rest of the community, I looked at my cabbages and I remembered the hunger I had subjected them to. What did she want? Why had she come to see me when Sikoeun was away?

The caress on my back, the bait of food—it reeked of a trap. Angkar controlled its proletarians by means of food. People would be brought to their knees for a bowl of broth. Being exploited was hard, certainly, but I preferred it to being one of the exploiters. I put the package in a cupboard, picked up my yoke and buckets, and continued my work.

The next day, one of Roeun's servants brought more bread, still warm and wonderfully appetizing. I took the bread and placed it in the cupboard, next to the other one. As night fell, I went to give the two loaves to Granny-cakes, not because she needed them, but I wanted proof that I had not bitten into the poisonous trap.

One morning, as I passed the courtyard in front of the children's house, I saw a child stretched face down on the ground. No one else was around. The child is dead! I thought to myself.

Then my blood froze in my veins. Paralyzed with fear, I ran to the body as quickly as my legs allowed me. I had recognized my older daughter.

"Narén! Narén!" I cried uncontrollably. Soon I felt her thin arms around me. "Sweetheart, what happened?" I asked, trying to loosen her tight embrace as she snuggled against my chest. It was then that I saw that her face was blue. "What happened?" I repeated.

Stubbornly, Narén clung to me. I talked to her gently, without probing into why she had been cast inert in the middle of the courtyard. I told her she was courageous and begged her to hold on at any cost.

· *Six* ·

In Cambodia, every full moon between the new year and the end of February is a time of spectacular fishing on the Tonle Sap ("Great Lake"—a natural flood reservoir of the lower Mekong and its distributaries). During this period, the barges return with ton after ton of fish.

At the beginning of the new year, people talked about it excitedly. Roeun organized expeditions to the lake so that foreigners could see the spectacle and witness the abundance of this resource. She also sent truckloads of fish to us, ordering us to eat or preserve them.

Everyone was mobilized to scale and gut the fish. Here, *prahok*—fermented fish—was prepared; there, bamboo was split to make skewers for smoking fish. Farther on, people were crushing and grinding salt. Racks on which to smoke fish were erected in the middle of the garden. All available jars were requisitioned to hold fish sauce. A festive atmosphere reigned; people ate their fill and in the evening worked late, burning mounds of leaves to fight the mosquitoes.

It was during this period that the first "disappearance" occurred. While we were all at work one night, I made a remark about Sien An's absence. In this closed world, there was no such thing as departing unnoticed. Nor could anyone escape the task assigned to him by Angkar.

The next day, while I was treating her with acupuncture, Granny-cakes told me that Sian An had had a heart attack and his wife had been called urgently to his side. Information from Granny-cakes was like a command. One had to believe it and repeat it in exactly the same way.

To learn more, I went to Sien An's room. There, everything was upside down, including the bed and the table, as if there had been a struggle. The closet was empty and the floor was scattered with photographs. The snapshots were of their children, dates carefully written on the back. I recognized Kourk, the youngest, nude and smiling on a pillow, and Nika, their other child. I had known Nika in Peking, where she behaved like a true little mistress of the house. When her parents went away, it was she who watched the pocketbook and knew how to make her brother obey.

What had happened to the couple? I couldn't find out anything more.

Then Moch's baby fell ill. It had been a long time since I visited her—not for lack of time but for lack of courage, and for fear of being exposed. Feeling remorse, I finally called on her. She was a woman who had reached the end of her physical and moral strength. She had never recuperated from giving birth and was exhausted by the daily chores. Moreover, she was constantly subjected to harassment.

"Wives of the people can expect no one to help them and must keep on carrying yokes of water after giving birth," she was told. "How dare you eat Angkar's rice? Do you think you are going to raise children without doing anything, as in the former society?"

Moch had difficulty getting medicine for the child. Her requests were answered with: "What do you expect from

Angkar, when you do nothing for Angkar? In the old society, doctors of your class did not care for the poor."

I suggested digging up some carrots so that she could prepare a bouillon. She agreed but was afraid. We risked being accused of taking things that belonged to Angkar.

After washing the carrots, I carefully cut off the tops to give to the rabbits. (The first rabbits had been brought to Bl by Sien An, who took care of them and saw to it that they reproduced rapidly. After his departure—one only spoke of "departures"—Phât, a coworker, had taken over. When he saw me with the carrot tops, he looked frightened. "Heaven spare me! What are you going to give them? Do you know that the traitor, Sien An, found a way of poisoning them before he left?")

The baby's condition deteriorated. By the time Angkar sent a motorbike and doctor to hospitalize the child, it was already too late.

When Moch cried for her baby, the elders mocked her lack of self-control. Two days later, she disappeared with her second son. No one knew what had happened to her. Moch's departure was presented as a charitable gesture toward someone who "could not keep up with the headlong development of the revolution."

Little by little, discussion seemed to center on Sien An's elimination. No one knew why, but references harked back often to Angkar's clearheadedness, obscure though it was to everyone. The only possible explanation was the emphasis placed on a new theme in ideological work: "In not running fast enough, we allow ourselves to be passed by!"

Once the process of eliminating the tardy ones began, the pace of events quickened. Several days later, while I was peeling vegetables in the kitchen with the other women, an elder approached and asked, in a lowered voice, to talk to Duong Som Ol and Sarin Chhak's wives.

In keeping with the current practice of secrecy, they stood apart and exchanged a few words. Then the two women went to their rooms. Five minutes later, as I left the kitchen after work, I saw a jeep on the street. Wary of being witness to something unusual, I hid and watched what was about to take place. I saw Sarin Chhak's wife get into the jeep with her bundle and watched the vehicle drive off.

That night, I questioned Sikoeun about the incident. "Sarin Chhak and Duong Som Ol are too old," he told me. "They could no longer follow or understand. It is best to take them out of circulation and thus avoid their becoming traitors."

At the end of January, Roeun, who was about to give birth to a sixth or seventh child, had an unusually high fever. She came frequently to Bl—as often as twice a day—distributing fruits, sugar, or orders. But what more could she have expected from us? She was already the mistress of the area and all of the team leaders were her nieces, nephews, and cousins. But then Roeun disappeared, and the members of her clan were sent on an "assignment." "She has been transferred to the countryside," it was rumored in Bl.

When Sar disappeared, we dared for the first time to whisper the word *purge*.

Ieng Sary named Vén as Roeun's replacement. Once promoted, Vén began to take privileges. She stopped eating at the canteen and wore smart clothes under her black outfit.

Roun, who had been team leader of the group of furniture movers, was replaced by a man named Houn. Originally from a remote minority group, he still expressed himself poorly in Khmer and was astonished at his sudden promotion.

Having seen trucks only from a distance, Houn categorically refused to get into the cab. Briskly climbing onto the roof, he sat cross-legged, arms folded, staring straight ahead, as if on the back of an elephant.

Houn was the one who decided to raise chickens on a large scale to provide meat for the group. We cleared an immense area of ripening manioc and built a huge chicken coop. Once the work was done, a pickup truck brought a hundred or so chickens and roosters. Then there was the problem of feeding them. We had to either reduce our own rations or let the fowl find their own food, which would have been far from beneficial to the crops.

Houn decided to put all of the chickens into the coop temporarily. It was a hot day, and by evening, when he went to look at his brood, he could count the survivors on one hand. The dead chickens went the way of the diplomatic store.

While awaiting my own fate, I resolutely cultivated my crops on the stony path. Thus, at the beginning of January, I had planted several rows of mint, radishes, carrots, cabbages, and lettuce. End to end, my rows would have measured more than two-hundred meters by eighty centimeters. To transport soil as well as to water the garden, I made dozens of trips under my yoke. One day, out of curiosity, I weighed a load of soil: forty kilos!

When I had finished preparing the ground, I cleared a gully along the path and planted tomatoes in the fine silt of the topsoil. I had the best tomatoes in the unit.

All of this, however, was not "my" field, nor were they "my" crops. But from it I derived one valuable source of strength: self-confidence. In judging myself by nature's yardstick, I came to know myself better.

In the morning, I continued to translate, even though my evenings made me want to abandon the effort. I looked for subtle meanings, just the right words, strong expressions.

The dry season became more severe in February. Under the colorless sky and burning sun, the hot air stung the skin and tightened every fiber in the body. Vegetation withered;

the watering holes had long since dried up. Among the crops, only my tomatoes flourished, favored by their location. Workers came to pick them every day, weighing them and recording the harvest in a book. There was no reason to keep such an account, but I was happy to see that these young people, recently illiterate, were able to keep a notebook.

It became urgent to reorganize the watering system. The wells, whose depths were reached by shaky, slippery planks, no longer sufficed. The time seemed propitious for digging a small reservoir; the office workers prepared to go into action. A plan was made: the pond would be twelve meters square by twelve meters deep. More convenient wooden ladders would be built, and bindweed and turtles would be placed in the well. We would plant citronella all around as a nesting place for the turtles.

The time came for construction of a large work site. Neon lights were installed and loudspeakers connected. I joined in the work, and by five o'clock, almost everyone was on the premises. In the dark of the night, the lights gave the paths of the garden the look of a large industrial site. It was magnificent. Everyone was in high spirits as they worked.

For the intellectuals constructing the work site, this manual labor was not the work of peasants. Nor was it a punishment or a sporting exercise. All of us equal, working together in the soil, intellectuals and combatants alike, we were transformed into companions, elevated by a feeling of pure joy. I was happy—insignificant and all-important at the same time, both a drop of water and the entire sea . . .

The next-to-last Saturday in February, at the sound of the first notes announcing the morning radio broadcast, I put down my yoke to go, as I did every day, to make sure that all tools were accounted for. I arranged the tools and ran my head and feet under the water while listening to the program broadcast over the loudspeakers. To my surprise, I realized that the radio was rebroadcasting yesterday's program. That had never happened before. Was it a technical problem? (I found out much later that the entire radio team had been arrested for undermining moral standards!)

The next day, Toch and Vanna returned from work in mid-afternoon, which was unusual. For some time, it had been rumored that they were on their way up and were going to be named ambassadors. Assuming that the decision had been made, I went to say my farewells. Vanna was very happy. "We are going to the country," she told me.

Speculation on their future was thus confirmed. They were going to visit several other regions before going abroad. In less than five minutes, they had packed their belongings. A jeep was already waiting for them. Vanna left without saying good-bye to her children, conforming to the new practice. I secretly admired them both. We had been friends for ten years.

I watched the car drive away and remained in the road a long time after the cloud of dust had settled. Then I found myself alone again.

The next day, Sikoeun exclaimed, "Ah, what a traitor, this Toch! He acknowledged nothing in front of the great Ieng Sary who, all the same, generously offered him a chance. He acted proud! But, once arrived at Security, he admitted everything outright. Ah, the traitor!"

March passed, and we started to speculate on events. Some claimed that Roeun and her clan were gathered in a reeducation camp in Takhmao. Others said—although no one dared to believe it—that they had all been shot, including the children.

At the child-care center, living conditions had improved considerably. Angkar had provided new clothes and more regular nourishment. The children also had regained their healthy complexion. Once more they were laughing, running, and jumping.

Thirteen months before, I had left my daughters, saying, "Good-bye—see you tonight!" Our situation had become so desperate, in this month of March, that I had the feeling of being reborn into another world.

By now the children's community at B1 had been reduced by half, which bore witness to the severity of the purge.

My girls soon tested the slightly loosened discipline. One day they came halfway to my house, and the next day even closer, driven by curiosity to see where I lived. Finally, Narén boldly asked to spend the night with me.

When they were inside, I pushed a table against the door. Their father was away and I was concerned: If our lives were threatened, would I know how to protect these precious beings? I asked myself.

How they had changed! How they had matured! In my presence, they abandoned Khmer behavior, its reserve and silence, as if taking off a coat, and became animated. They were now five and six years old. I had missed seeing them grow!

They opened the closet to see what was inside, examined the bath and the sliver of soap I had saved for months, resisting using it to the end. They knowingly sniffed it to confirm that the children received better-smelling soap!

As we talked, sitting on the bed, Sokha got up, went in search of a glass of water, and placed the glass between us. "We share this in common," she said.

In their joy and excitement, Narén and Sokha played and talked until the early morning. Our hearts beat in unison in the happiness of being together again. Neither the past nor the future mattered. We were happy.

When the loudspeakers in the garden broadcast the station signal for the first radio broadcast, they splashed water on their faces and left, running hand in hand like a flight of ethereal fairies.

*　　*　　*

During the seminars that took place in early April for the second anniversary of the liberation, Ieng Sary again took over the position that in the past he had given Roeun.

The celebration was particularly solemn and formal. I was invited to one of the sessions.

For several hours, I listened to discussions of the purges that had taken place over the last couple of weeks. Five "major traitors" had been eliminated: Koy Thoun, president of the Northern Zone, and his clan; Soeu Doeun, secretary of state for commerce; Roeun's husband, Toch Phoeun; Sien An, the president of the Pochentong airport, and his wife Krean Lean; Sean Layni and his wife—all people I had known, appreciated, or admired. (What Ieng Sary failed to mention during his account was that before sending them to Security, he had announced a promotion to each of them!)

Once he had finished talking, Ieng Sary became solemn and asked the participants to collaborate in denouncing these "traitors."

Several people demanded a word. One complained about not having been able to marry, another worked too hard, others couldn't visit their homes in the countryside, despite promises that had been made to them. Rone spoke emotionally of her mother, whom she had left for three days—two years ago. Each complaint ended with a rousing: "Long live Angkar! Down with the traitors!"

Then a combatant began to criticize the last statement Roeun had made just before her arrest. Ieng Sary interrupted the soldier, saying that Angkar's statements were always righteous. There was a long silence . . . No one knew what to think.

Once the seminar was over, everyone imagined that better days lay ahead—when they would be able to marry, see their families, work less, learn more, and so on.

For the anniversary of the liberation, a great banquet was organized, the first in two years. A pig was stuffed, and that night everyone enjoyed themselves.

Among the young people, Kalyane, Vanna's daughter, ran and laughed cheerfully. (Vanna had been a politician when Sihanouk was in power.) "Too bad they aren't here to enjoy themselves with us," Kalyane declared in the general excitement, thinking of her parents, who were still officially in the countryside.

Choeun, the team leader at B1, heard the remark. An hour later, a car came for Kalyane and her brother. They were taken to a subunit of B1 that was devoted to vegetable and livestock production. From morning to night, one watched the animals, the other watered the vegetables. When they returned to B1, they didn't dare look at their old friends or say a word about what had happened.

Boasting about having cleansed its internal branches, Angkar established plans for national reconstruction.

According to Angkar, by the very structure of things, given the transfer of property to the state, agriculture and industry already belonged to the future. The problem of production had yet to be resolved, however, and in order to advance more rapidly, plodding buffalo and handcarts would need to be replaced by trucks. The idea was presented as something original.

Transportation would be modernized within five years, agriculture within ten, and industry within twenty. A new wind drove the movement. All hopes were still possible.

Various activities were reorganized. Garden plots would be extended, and pigs, ducks, rabbits, pigeons, and even turtles would be raised. Vén procured some sugarcane and assigned me to plant it—something new that pleased me. We were supposed to plant twice as much eggplant as last year . . . Our production was expected to increase rapidly.

* * *

After more than six months at B1, only one of the four garden workers, Bien, had moved to a job in an office. The others were still being put to the test. One of them admitted timidly that he found the living conditions too harsh and asked to return to his family. His request shocked many people; even more astonishing was Angkar's positive response.

The day after his departure, the garden was empty. The two other young workers didn't come all day. Or the next day. No one had any news of them, but it was rumored that they had been implicated in a plot against Angkar.

Then it was Heng Pich's turn. He was one of the people responsible for moving and transportation. Small, thin, and bald, with eyes like slits, Heng Pich had been a former general in the army under Sihanouk.

Heng Pich was accused of economic sabotage. The redistribution of furniture of bourgeois Phnom Penh houses was suddenly considered a counterrevolutionary act, a waste evaluated at hundreds of thousands of dollars! No explanation was given for this sudden change of policy, but the movings stopped and Heng Pich disappeared.

The scope and number of accusations of plots against Angkar was dizzying. The whole family of the accused—brothers, sisters, cousins, nephews, wives, children (even newborns)—were charged with the same crime. In addition, all who had approached these so-called traitors, from near or afar, were considered part of the network organized by the accused. To have been at a meal or a meeting together or even to have smiled while shaking hands was proof of complicity. "We act in the name of purity," said Angkar. "We must totally root out the evil. One bad grain can give the whole field bad weeds."

Angkar congratulated itself on its understanding, audacity, and will to wipe out all of the traitors for the good

97

of the people. This provoked laudatory comments from the combatants: "Angkar must truly love the people to turn in cadres it had patiently trained over the years. Long live Angkar, which protects us against foreign plots."

The elimination of spy networks depended on "avowals and confessions" drafted by the accused. Each individual charged had to retrace his life, reconstruct events, and recall names of people known, met, or contacted. Lists of one hundred or two hundred names were common. Any person whose name appeared on three of these lists was arrested. Later, given the incredible number of arrests resulting from this method, the number was raised to five.

Sikoeun told me Ieng Sary had warned him that he had been denounced three times. He also told me of a dinner he had been invited to, following Phnom Penh's liberation, to share a kilo of noodles retrieved in one of the moves. He had accepted the invitation but then was unable to attend. Now the meal was considered to have been a planning meeting for a plot against the state!

Everyone was pressured and strongly encouraged to denounce traitors. Denouncing your friends could be a way to protect yourself, but it also meant taking the risk of them doing the same, without any assurance that Angkar would put a higher price on your word than on theirs.

Sikoeun continued to harass me. He wanted me to confess that I had contact with the KGB, the CIA, the French intelligence service, and Vietnamese agencies!

Had I not seen so many friends slip away, I would have laughed at these accusations. But an atmosphere of general suspicion had swept over B1, and I was alone, powerless. I could not let myself be upset. I had to strengthen my will and remain vigilant. Stubbornly, I followed my normal routine, concealing my fright. I knew that I was being observed and that the slightest deviation on my part would be interpreted as proof of my guilt.

The logic used to detect the guilty was a combination

of pseudopsychoanalysis and calculated suffering. Those who had nothing to hide did everything perfectly, without fault. The guilty were necessarily impelled to do something that would reveal their depravity. Several elders were literally pale with fright.

All alone, Mi launched madly into hoeing a huge parcel of land. He must have had much on his conscience! His strange behavior fed every suspicion. And Bien, the chief of protocol, took off his white shirt to scrape the septic tanks clean . . .

Keat Chhon and Thiounn Prasith never left each other's side. We saw them sauntering, heads down, backs arched, tormented by anxiety.

As for Phât, he was terrified. His wife had been Roeun's assistant. She had escaped the dragnet thus far but was probably serving as bait. Phât took care of the rabbits. As long as they were healthy, he would be left alone—but let him beware if they took sick!

That is why he arrived at my building one day in a state of frenzy. It appeared that the eyes of his rabbits had begun to swell. I went with him to inspect the animals but could only confirm what Phât feared: myxomatosis, a viral disease usually fatal to rabbits. He went to great lengths to find sugar and managed to keep the illness in check. But in the end, the rabbits died. Phât, his wife, and their infant, only a few weeks old, disappeared.

The same happened to Bien, whom I saw departing one day as usual on the back of a motorcycle. His wife, then six months pregnant, had suspected nothing.

The wives of those who disappeared were never told what lay in store for their husbands. Their hopes remained alive a long time before they learned the hard truth. This often occurred in an indirect way. For example, in keeping with the tradition that the name of the first child be a synthesis of the parents' names, Von's wife named the baby Vong. One day, Hong suggested she give the child another name. This was how she learned that she would never see her husband again.

Shocking news came from every unit, from every region, citing instances of schemes and plots. The wave of purges, which until a few months before were thought to be limited to one unit and one clan, now swept through the whole country. Cambodia, it was said, was infested with international subversion. Each person was pegged as an enemy in power. Only those who followed Angkar's plans and beliefs to the letter were free of suspicion.

Through the inquiries that were made public, we learned that Toch Kam Doeun's crime was that he expressed an opinion during a meeting. The same was true for Sien An.

After these purification purges, which were regarded as a beneficial bloodletting, Ieng Sary called together several top leaders and their families from the northwestern region, which was led by Sou. After a short stay at B1, they were sent to a special unit to prepare to go abroad to open embassies. Several days later, however, we learned that they were considered traitors.

We were astonished to learn that popular elders, who we liked and thought of as parents, were taking part in conspiracies. All good yesterday, in one fell swoop the cadres were all bad today.

I was told one day to move into a building occupied by young couples. Then, one night after dinner, Sikoeun solemnly announced that I had been asked to go to the office at 8:00 P.M. I asked no questions and arrived punctually.

There, I was ushered into a room in which, in accordance with the new custom, a group of people were seated, working around the same table. The whole general affairs and information section was there: Mi, Mân, Saê, Pin, Roeth, and Khon.

As I sat down, Saê started talking. "My respects to all

of the elders present! I declare the meeting open. This evening we will hear comrade Phâl's profound revolutionary confession."

So that was it! I thought. Taken unawares and annoyed at having stumbled into such a common trap, I smiled to hide my confusion and to stall for some time. Then I threw myself into the game, playing the card of sincerity. I declared that as the daughter in a working-class family, I knew the hardships of the exploited and that I wholeheartedly shared all of the efforts of the Khmer people. I briefly pointed out that I had learned a lot in so little time and that I was doing my best to "structure myself." At the end of my statement, I mentioned my desire to become modest, according to Angkar's will. Then, with a big smile, I announced that I was done.

I had not talked long. I did not have the rhetorical gift of the others, who were able to develop one redundancy after another and stretch out their talks over hours. As it turned out, though, I was far from finished. Each person in turn, choosing different themes, delivered a long peroration about me. "You were born and grew up in a country that exploited and murdered our people for over a century. You are, by your very nature, colonialist! . . .

"You have been a part of the French worker's world. The French worker's movement is totally dependent on the Soviet Union. You therefore have revisionist tendencies. . . .

"You have admired and supported the Vietnamese war of resistance at the same time that Vietnam was stabbing us in the back. . . .

"You like China and don't hide it. But China is not a real friend, she wants to colonize us. . . .

"You think about your mother too much. You don't see the bad influence she has on you. . . .

"You think about your children too much. You don't see the problems you cause them."

After everyone had finished and I was given the floor, I did not defend myself. The session had lasted two and a half hours.

I went back to my room with a splitting headache. The next day I came down with a fever. Nevertheless, I went to the office, as usual, with my translations. The workers cast side-glances toward me, observing the session's effects.

All day I wandered in circles, lost in thought. How can I be what they want me to be without losing myself? I wondered. They can take everything from me, but I cannot disown my mother or abandon my daughters! Angkar demands that I stop being my own master. To be free, to be one's own master, was considered counterrevolutionary.

"One must strike while the iron is hot," people liked to say about the "new" (former city dwellers forced to evacuate to the countryside). A week later, I was again put in the hot seat. I had nothing new to say, but the gathering itself had much to teach me. Following the same scenario, each person spoke:

"Comrade Phâl tries, but she always acts like people of her race. We have chased the French away, but they still covet our country. In her manner, in her way of talking, walking, sitting, the comrade remains French—"

"It is not my fault," I interrupted, "if my physical build does not enable me to squat."

"You answer almost anything, no matter when, no matter how," I was told. "That is also typical of your race. Our women are modest. They listen modestly, without saying anything. They do as they are told to do. . . .

"You always arrange things your own way, you don't take into account our opinions and our observations. You pretend that 'six of one and half a dozen of the other' are the same thing. But they are not the same thing! We are putting you on guard against your counterrevolutionary obstinacy. . . .

"In France, people cling to their personality. The more

102

personality, the better. This personality shaped in comrade Phâl since her tender childhood is a hard shell. She will have a lot of trouble getting rid of it. It will be a downright surgical operation she will have to conduct on herself, a very painful operation. . . ."

To close, Sikoeun spoke for twenty minutes. He accused me of everything—from my mother whom I cared about too much to my children whose skin color too clearly marked their imperialist origins. He spoke at length about things from the past and recalled details even I had forgotten. He reproached me for my way of working and for how little attention I paid to corrections made on my translations.

Then he announced his suspicions: that I might belong to one or more foreign spy rings. "Foreigners are patient," he concluded. "They infiltrate certain elements and lie low before pulling off a big coup. If comrade Phâl didn't have all of this nostalgia for the past, she wouldn't make so many typing mistakes in her translations."

I kept a grip on myself to keep from crying.

The meeting ended late. Leaving the office, I looked at the sky, the moon, and the stars shining in the crisp evening. I took a deep breath. In the child-care center, a light burned. The rooster crowed already—or was it again . . .

I breathed in the immensity of the sky and, just as I had done as a little girl, said, "When I grow up, I will travel. I'll see new horizons. . . ."

· *Seven* ·

In mid-September, an air of excitement seemed to liven up the offices. I was asked to give a hand to a group of young people working in isolation on the upper floor. They were making banners. Squatting girls pasted down the cardboard letters with glue made of boiled rice: "Long live the Communist party of Kampuchea," the banners said. The scene surprised me, because the past celebrations of the party had been restrained.

We made banners for the next several days, working late into the evening. One night, Hong brought bread, fruit, coffee, and milk. It was the first time that these young people tried coffee—a very strong brew. An hour later, they were all stretched out, hearts palpitating, trying to give one another rubdowns with Tiger Balm.

Each group of workers was officially informed that the 1977 Communist party festival would be celebrated openly. It would be a big event, with international repercussions. Indeed, the Khmer revolution had only one precedent: the October Revolution.

Everyone was supposed to be involved in the festivities and learn to sing "The International." The text was typed in the office and then distributed to all of the teams. From morning till night, one could hear the song echo throughout the camp, arousing an emotion even more powerful than that felt by starving bodies anticipating the banquet.

Trucks came in succession, bringing all kinds of food: rice, manioc, orange drink, meat. The atmosphere warmed up and people became animated. During the festivities, there was plenty of food. Everyone was jubilant. For much less, we could have forgotten the past! We thought we had finally seen the light at the end of the tunnel.

We were taken to a theater performance in the Bassac style—a traditional, lyrical style. It was the first such performance since the liberation. The radio reported that delegations from all over the country were attending. The performance was held at nine in the morning. We got up before daybreak and walked in rank to the site. As we arrived, we were carefully searched—women on one side, men on the other. "Too often, during the war, spectators became so caught up in the action that they shot at the actors. . . ." we were told, in explanation of this measure. The acting was good, the set was well done, the voices effortless, and the songs magnificent. What a beautiful spectacle it was!

The banquet brought a sense of well-being and fulfillment to our underfed bodies and inspired gratitude toward the generous donors.

It was typical of Angkar to use food as a weapon. At work sites, young people received a food ration for each day of work. If they fell sick, they received only a little clear broth, which incited them to work regardless of their health. From time to time, after a more arduous task, sweet bouillon was distributed. This had not only a physical but a psychological effect on their weakened bodies. Hunger haunted all of our thoughts, although we didn't want to admit it, even to ourselves.

Our bodies could not help but be grateful to Angkar, which we had been ordered henceforth to call the party.

Its political line was correct and clairvoyant. We had to say it and believe it firmly, which we did.

It was at this time of party glorification that I was officially introduced at the office. "The party long ago decided to put you to work in the offices," Saê told me, "but Sikoeun opposed it."

I settled in with Mân and Roeth in an office next to Sikoeun's where all of the typing and copying machines were to be found. There, every day, we received direct transcripts of the radio broadcasts. We could also quickly type, run off, and mail the daily bulletin. Mailings abroad went out weekly on the Saturday flight. The embassy in Peking took care of sending the mailings onward.

Criticism sessions intensified at the rate of two nights per week. During these meetings, it seemed that each person's past, far from being a tapestry of complex motives, could be reduced to a straight line pointing inevitably toward either service to the party or treason.

The most harmless facts now assumed high political significance. A lack of speed in executing a task demonstrated a sabotage mentality. Zeal was an undeniable sign of longing for power.

Thoughts had as much value as actions. To be on the right track, one had to imbue oneself with the ideas of the party in such a way that the mind was perpetually mobilized to the party's service, without hesitation and without wasting time, like a machine.

"In terms of discipline, I have some shortcomings," one heard. "I didn't listen to the radio transmissions with all of the required concentration." (Listening to the radio had become obligatory; each of us had to pay close attention to the broadcasts so as to be able to comment on them later.) Or, "I urinated outside the manure bin. . . ."

The elders orchestrated the confessions with a masterly hand. They started the movement and then let it develop, intervening only to require more sincerity if they judged that the words were turning into the same old story. The choice of "interrogators" was not made in advance, and the elders decided on the spot who would be questioned. Those who "evolved well" were left alone, while particular attention was given to those who "went bad."

Listening to these accounts of facts and signals, people searched for signs of weakness. Language was analyzed and psychoanalyzed. Each of the "mistaken actions" underwent interpretation. One bulletin badly stapled, printed, or typed became an indicator—if not actual proof—of secret conspiracies.

Roeth was one of those who was put through the ringer. His former colleagues were arrested, resulting in his innocence being questioned. A hustler and a handyman, Roeth knew how to do a lot of things, but none of them well. He had been asked to do all of the minor tasks regarding electricity, mechanics, and even cabinetmaking. He was both exploited and scorned.

He was continually criticized in public remarks and remonstrances, which only served to increase his anxiety and provoke a growing feeling of inadequacy.

He was soon accused of working for the KGB and the Vietnamese. Driven into a corner, Roeth broke down. He started crying, which excited his critics: with a clear conscience, one does not let oneself be shaken!

Roeth confessed: influenced by a comrade, he had cut a piece of sugarcane which he had then eaten in secret.

"Economic crime!" came the accusation.

He also confessed that he would have liked to get married.

"Corrupt thinking!"

But he added that he wanted to serve the party with all his power and dedicated himself to it completely, body and soul. The party excused him and left him alone.

Relieved, Roeth took up his work with that much more

speed and care. The party soon informed him that it was arranging for him to marry a young woman he had known long ago.

Things were nicely done. A small villa was cleaned, the same villa where Moch had been married. Sweets and fruit were brought. Designated guests arrived late at night. They modestly refused the food. Few spoke. The atmosphere was uneasy. After the ceremony, everyone left on their own. The couple was given two days' rest—the first time such a privilege had been accorded. But the next day, at 5:00, Roeth was watering the vegetables as usual. Then he stayed at the office until 8:00. No one could reproach him for his zeal, as everything he did was strictly in order.

Coming into the kitchen one morning, I found the women flustered. The basket of corn had disappeared! Certain of having left it on a stand, they questioned themselves about this unusual disappearance. Then, noticing that the door had been forced, they speculated, "Maybe it's only the boys, during their night watch duty. . . ."

Then, two days later, a fellow from the team in charge of rubberizing roofs to prevent leaks, came to the kitchen and asked what a basket of corn was doing on the building's roof! He was astonished and amused. The women jumped: the lost basket!

Just two couples lived in the building. The men worked at the office. The couples were brought in for their self-criticism and, unaware of the discovery of the basket of corn, gave their usual accounts. Then, when the meeting should have broken up, the president permitted a long silence before asking, "Have you never wanted to eat corn?"

One of the men turned red and, annoyed, declared, "Seeing the corn ripen in the garden, I was tempted to grill an ear. . . ."

"And so?"

"Once, I picked one to grill it and eat it. . . ." The man appeared more and more troubled. At fifty years old, confessing a weakness of this kind in front of twelve people is certainly uncomfortable.

"So. And the basket of corn, what do you plan to do with it?"

The two couples were given lesser tasks, and their position in the community became untenable. People pointed at them and refused to speak to them. Finally they were informed of the party's mercy: they would leave the next day to join their children in the countryside for a few days.

A week later, they still had not returned. In the kitchen, people already knew the couples' fate. "They must have been hungry to drink so much water!" people said. "They must have been traitors to have been so hungry!"

Along with the dry season, the northwesterly breezes began to blow, and work in the garden picked up again.

Like the peasants in the cooperatives, we produced our own manure—which is why the very early hours of the day found me walking downstairs with a bucket of urine in hand. Climbing the stairs to the offices, our throats gagged at the natural-ammonia smell. The men relieved themselves in a small pot. By the time the pot was full, the first urine had begun to decompose. One can imagine the odor!

People at the office were very proud of this practice. Ieng Sary himself never passed up a chance to add his contribution. All of this was, apparently, excellent for revolutionary morale!

I liked being the first to reach the garden in the morning. I lit the big lights. It was so beautiful! I felt a great sense of liberation. I especially liked it when the sky was reddening and the struggle began between the red and the black. The red ended up chasing the black but at the same time disappeared from the light.

At the moment the light triumphed, a sublime instant among us, the banana trees moved their leaves and the sugarcane began to rustle. The earth saluted the light. It was the eternal, joyous song of the renewal of life.

As the year ended, we heard the first rumors of border fighting against the Vietnamese. I learned of the news in the kitchen, where they were grinding salt in preparation for the next loads of fish. Battles were described in great detail. People said the hospital was full of wounded. Yet we had heard of this situation neither on the radio nor in the hallways of the ministry.

Arriving at the office on New Year's Day, I learned that everyone had been waiting for the printing of a very important document. They were just adding the last touches before dispatching a box of letters and papers. The car waited to take it and deliver it to the plane, which was supposed to take off immediately. Through the half-open door, I saw Sikoeun get up, staggering before the typewriter. Sugarcane debris littered the floor. He had just finished working for two days and two nights at a stretch.

Once the box was dispatched, I was told with great pride about the document. When the international press gets wind of it, people said, the world would be astonished. It was a declaration announcing the Vietnamese aggression and a proclamation by the party of the rupture of diplomatic relations.

"We got them first!" people exclaimed. "When the world hears the news, it will jump!"

Everyone was thinking war. Hours later, we officially learned that there was intense fighting on Cambodian land. The next day we were told that our troops had inflicted heavy losses on the enemy.

Propaganda efforts were stepped up, and meetings were organized in which each person "vehemently denounced crimes committed by the enemy." All agreed that we had to "crush the Vietnamese."

While battles raged on the front, in Phnom Penh the fish were plentiful. Huge loads of it were brought in trucks. Everyone was mobilized to prepare the pickling brine. In the evening, we ate fried fish cakes, the *prahit*.

One morning, we were surprised by sounds that became louder and louder. The rumblings made the building tremble. Three big armored cars passed on the street. A briefing followed; we were told that the armored cars were returning from the front after having destroyed the Vietnamese.

Historic victory! Total victory! Thanks to the clairvoyant party line, the fighting was finished almost as soon as it began. It was announced that our daily rice ration would be increased and that from now on, two dishes would be served at each meal. Cries of victory intensified. "Meanwhile," they reminded us, "the worst enemy remains the enemy within."

And the witch-hunt took off again, worse than ever.

In the hospitals, the situation was less brilliant and the victory was not trumpeted in the same way. There were many wounded. An appeal for blood was launched. Young people volunteered en masse, but the program did not last, to our general astonishment. We soon learned that the medical personnel in charge of transfusions were tragically incompetent. Newly recruited and trained on the job, after the first contingent of revolutionary doctors were gone, these people had made even greater errors and caused many unnecessary deaths.

The diplomats who had been stationed in Vietnam soon returned. Cheang and Touch, the ambassadors, seemed surprised by the changes in everyday life at B1 and were astounded by developments in the collectivist regime since their departure eighteen months earlier. Although exhausted by war and guerrilla life, they were overtaken by the strength and breadth of the movement.

The couple was also unaware of all of the purges. The news shocked them. From day to day, they changed their outlook and their behavior. Their sense of satisfaction and triumph upon their arrival was replaced by incomprehension and then concern. One afternoon, Touch spoke to me in the kitchen. I did not understand what she wanted to tell me, but I was struck by the tone in her voice. She was choking with tears.

That night, Cheang and Touch disappeared. At the meeting, they were accused of being accomplices and of being responsible for Vietnamese aggression, the thousands of dead, and the destruction.

At the beginning of the year, B1 welcomed a large contingent of children from the countryside. Thin, without any baggage, and barefoot, they had never before seen a town. They had no idea what faucets or light switches were used for. The party dressed them and sent them to school.

Manuals were edited (first a geography book, then a reader) and tasks and programs were set up. Three people were assigned full time to their training.

Progress was very quick, people said, despite the low level of understanding of the children, who were used to a very simple life. In addition to their regular schooling, they were ideologically trained. They quickly learned party terminology so that they might hold wise and boisterous discussions, just like the elders.

The children were told that the first generation of cadres had been treasonous and the second generation wasn't much better. Thus, they would soon be asked to take up the cause. The innocents would become young foxes. They would judge unsparingly their "uncles" and "aunts" and treat them without respect, going so far as to eat from their plates if they so desired.

It was among this new generation that the child doctors appeared. These girls, aged nine to thirteen, could hardly read, yet the party saw fit to confide a jar of syringes to each and designate them to give shots.

"Our child doctors," people said, "come from the peasants. They are ready to serve their class. They are remarkably intelligent. Tell them the red jar contains vitamins, and they'll remember it! Show them how to sterilize a syringe and they'll know how to do it!"

These children were unquestionably pure-hearted, but there was a certain recklessness that accompanied the knowledge of how to administer shots. In a very short time, the child doctors began to demonstrate unprecedented arrogance and insolence.

Gradually, as the number of workers increased, the canteen was extended to the two festival halls, but the time came to restructure the kitchen as well.

The new kitchen was built and organized on a scale appropriate to the collective. Several hallways were arranged and supplied with industrial-size kettles. Heating was done from outside. One person was in charge. The work was hard and the spectacle impressive: entire tree trunks were burned.

To cook rice, a system of eight stackable metal trays was adopted. Each tray was one meter in diameter and could hold five kilos of rice. A lid, more than a meter and a half long, attached to the ceiling by a pulley system, came to rest on the stack of trays. Forty kilos of rice could be cooked at once with this system. The rice served at the table, then, was warm, which everyone appreciated.

I was thrilled when the huge lid went down and up.

The pulley creaked, vapor escaped. The effect was like being in a small factory.

Another kitchen-factory improvement under study would provide boiled water at all times. Hygienically, water was the only drink allowed. It was a good rule, as fevers became increasingly rare.

This kitchen-factory was a small marvel, but I grew to miss the earlier days, when the atmosphere in the kitchen was more relaxed.

At the end of January, a new series of seminars was begun. I was invited as a full participant, but I did not appreciate the gesture as I would have two and a half years earlier. I no longer wanted to see myself integrated with the flock.

The seminar was held in a big room in the ministry near the area where negotiations were underway with a Thai delegation. Participants were asked to move about as quietly as possible to foster discipline.

During the course of his speech, Ieng Sary confirmed that internal affairs were now well cleansed. The spy networks had been decapitated. Relaxed and smiling, he announced that food would improve. From here on, pregnant and nursing women would have the right to a breakfast of leftovers.

As usual, the seminar ended with public confessions followed by criticisms and debates.

One afternoon, Ieng Sary came to visit workers in the garden. Preceded by bodyguards, he strode to the edge of the wet soil. I was at the far end watering the sugarcane when I heard him forcefully declare, "The Chinese had Norman Bethune. We, we have Aunt Phâl!"

Everyone felt they had to laugh. I remained confused. It was not the first time I had been compared to Bethune, but after the long months of hazing and humiliation, I did not know what to think.

On the path to the canteen, Sikoeun and the others complimented me. I smiled and said I was unworthy of the honor. I did not like the criticisms, but I was even more distrustful of this kind of attention. What to do? If I wanted to survive and hold on to a hope of escaping this trap, I would, at the risk of losing myself, have to follow the direction imposed on me.

After March, the heat returned, again putting us to the test. Vegetation was stunted, but industrial life improved. It could be seen in the increased road traffic and the number of trains arriving loaded with foul-smelling latex.

It was spring in Phnom Penh. For Sikoeun and me, it was a time of rediscovery. We were reunited in a new love whose force and joy were in proportion to the tests we had endured for the past two years.

Our gradually renewed love gave us confidence in the future. We felt strong enough to overcome the obstacles we would face. In the joy of this spring, I forgot the sufferings of the past. We left a hell in which many of our close friends remained engulfed, and lived our happiness as if drinking fresh water after crossing a desert.

When my daughters asked, "Mama, why didn't you come to get us when Noeun gagged us and beat us in the secret cabinet?" all I could say was, "All of that is over; our tomorrows will sing!"

To be honest, we had no idea what tomorrow would bring.

· *Eight* ·

As the third anniversary of Phnom Penh's liberation approached, Ieng Sary invited the diplomatic corps to view a film on the general situation in Cambodia. B1 was requested to fill the room and to applaud. I was put on guard to stay in the back of the room and not let myself be seen. I was just glad for the chance to leave the ministry compound.

The film showed the extent to which life in Democratic Kampuchea had become beautiful. Leaders were close to the people. We saw them all, in fact, pictured at the different bases, marching in step as if on parade, ranked in hierarchical order.

The film over, we started to file out when the projection room announced that it had just received a movie filmed by some Yugoslavian journalists who had visited at the start of the dry season in 1977. Although the sound track was missing, we watched a succession of images that presented a reality undeniably different from the official version. The terror that infused the scenes filmed in rural zones was clearly transmitted to the assembled spectators, all of whom were aware of the consequences that would flow from this diplomatic incident.

The projectionists were immediately arrested and accused of being part of a CIA network. I wondered what would happen to Sikoeun, since he had accompanied the film crew during its travels throughout Cambodia.

For the national festival commemorating the third anniversary of the Khmer Rouge victory, the seminar, usually organized in three cycles, was reduced to one. The second in command, Ieng Sary, had a lot of work and too many worries.

I was invited to a seminar one morning. We began by singing the national anthem and "The International." Then Ieng Sary spoke solemnly about the purge movement. This movement, which we thought was finished—that we would have loved to see finished—had continued! Foreigners had undermined the whole state, Ieng Sary declared. Two new spy rings had recently been dismantled. The first had been run by Van Piny.

Seizing a file put in front of him, Ieng Sary exclaimed, "His confessions are here." Ieng Sary then gave Van Piny's story. A CIA agent since his youth, he had patiently climbed the ladder to become chief of an important network. . . . Among other things, the man admitted to having wasted fifty coconuts.

"Fifty coconuts!" Ieng Sary repeated with an offended air. "That's economic sabotage!" Then he paused. On the corner of the table, there was a similar dossier. I awaited the finish.

Taking on an even more serious expression, he continued. "We have victoriously dismantled another network, a much more important one. The document that you see," he said, holding up the second dossier, "is made up of 150 written pages. These are confessions. The person who wrote them let us all down. He was the head of a network of 150 people, a CIA network first constituted in Phnom Penh and then in France. This man, who passed as a compatriot and a revolutionary, had gained the confidence of elders. But only to betray them! This man is Leang Sirivouth!"

Sirivouth! Sikoeun's cousin! I felt eyes staring at me. I could not believe it. If it had been hard for me to give credence to accusations against other people who had been close to me, when it came to Sirivouth, it was impossible!

I knew Sirivouth had to have been sentenced to death, but for my own survival I had to remain impassive.

The session continued. Ieng Sary assured us that after these latest arrests, only one highly placed traitor remained. To hear him, one got the idea that since he knew who the traitor was, he would do whatever was necessary to put an end to the purges—that he felt it was time to move on to concrete things. After all, at a time when troops were massing at the border weren't there better things to be done?

"The last traitor is up to you to find," Ieng Sary continued. "Heighten your revolutionary vigilance and denounce the person."

Immediately people began denouncing this and that. One person stood up to claim that he had noticed for a long time that the film projection team was a group of traitors. Someone else went one better. Then it was the young projectionist's wife, blushing with timidity, who took a turn at speaking out. She declared that she no longer recognized the father of her child, this "traitor who, by betraying the party, had deceived her." And finally Choeun intervened to lend support to his comrade's courageous position and give his personal assurances that the child would be raised by the highest principles and would become a solid defender of the country and the revolution.

The room began to boil. Ieng Sary spoke again: "We mustn't judge those who haven't already been judged."

The crowd became quiet. Everyone understood that the fires of criticism had to be directed outside the group. After a long pause, someone stood up and gave a harsh description of the situation in a manual labor camp in a suburb headed by Phoeun, Nane's husband, and Xean, who, along with his wife Sonn, was a cadre of Ieng Sary's generation. He claimed that the manual labor hours were too long and the ideological work inadequate. Someone else spoke up to recount how the ducks in the camp had died after being fed poisoned fish. After several others had made comments, Phoeun got up to speak. He spoke at length, taking a defensive position, which did not augur well. The pace of the accusations picked up again and the session continued until the start of the banquet.

The festivities lasted three days. But behind Phnom Penh's spring softness was a raging storm of purges. Vén was sent off with his two daughters, then Yane (even though she was seven months pregnant), her husband Doun, and some young teachers.

We were also told about the elimination of several provincial leaders. With no outside news about the combatants and lower cadres "placed in reeducation," one could expect only the worst for them. The drivers who journeyed around the country had not glimpsed them anywhere.

Three years after the revolution, it was necessary to go back to the beginning: everything had to be reorganized.

Priority was given to reopening the school. Ieng Sary brought in Voeun, a minority who served on the Central Committee, to direct the youth. His goal was to teach the major foreign languages so that he might train a contingent of reliable translators and interpreters.

Several adults from a neighboring camp were recruited as professors. Pin was chosen to teach English, Bunreth to teach Thai. I was put in charge of French, Spanish, and typing.

This nomination hardly delighted me. I had been at B1 long enough to know that the higher one was placed, the more easily one was struck down. Saê tried to tell me otherwise: "The party is showing great confidence in you. If it had believed that your thoughts and ideas could cast a shadow on the pure spirits of children, it would not have given you this responsibility. You should be thankful for the honor given to you. . . ."

In any case, I had no choice. I prepared, as best I could, various booklets to teach the languages and typing according to methods that seemed appropriate.

On top of my usual typing tasks, I had a huge amount of other work. The party, I sensed, was challenging me. With my new teaching load, my workday got heavier. At 5:00 A.M. I was in the garden. At 6:00 I started three hours of classes. At 9:00 I was at the office for the rest of the day.

I was on the job every day from six in the morning to midnight. For eighteen hours of work, I earned two meager portions of food.

I noticed a rose, in full bloom like a lotus flower at the top of a tree trunk. The rose exhaled a subtle perfume. The next morning I took a few minutes to stop in front of it and breathed deeply.

How I would have liked to be a flower!

Every morning before starting the first class, we had to sing the national hymn and "The International." I would stand up, my back turned to the class, and we would sing, arms extended along the body for the national hymn and with a fist raised for the other.

I didn't feel right about submitting to this ritual or imposing it on the children. It scared me to the point where, at the same time, I had to watch myself to keep from making a sign of the cross or genuflecting, as I had done at church when I was little.

The children's ideological training was intensive. Teaching was organized around the party and the gratitude each one owed it. The students ranged from nine to twelve years old. It was their first time in school, and some of the girls cried and begged for their mothers. No one knew how they had been selected to attend.

"Some cry for their mothers," it was said, "but can their mothers give them what the party does?"

"No!" the assembled children would shout in unison.

Other reorganizations paralleled the reopening of the schools. The hospital was equipped with a maternity ward, and pregnant women and women in childbirth were offered decent medical care.

The party wanted many children. It multiplied the marriages that were celebrated by ten, twenty, or thirty couples, at the rate of one batch per month. Choeun kept the register and a notebook on menstruations. Things moved quickly. People presented themselves as candidates, the party formed couples. The marriages took place in the hours that followed.

Married couples who worked in different units had little time together. Marriages were arranged to fall exactly during the woman's most fertile period. There was no place for poetry or sentiment. Once the woman was pregnant, the husband did not come back.

There were many new changes. It was like a mania. They wanted to group people according to their teams. The concept of compartmentalization motivated all changes.

Leaving work for lunch one day, I was informed that henceforth, I would be living at the very end of the row of buildings. Decisions were made and executed behind our backs under the direction of Choeun, who had a score to settle with the people at work.

*　　*　　*

Every morning I drank at the well of true happiness: on my way to class I made a habit of going by the child-care center. My daughters would run toward me: "Aunt," they would say, while the other children called me "mother." This was the height of absurdity, my being the aunt of my own children and the mother of others' children.

The children had been assembled in three groups. The youngest gathered in a nursery, where they were cared for with devotion. The others were turned over to a woman named Thi, who proved to have an exceptional mastery over the group. We never heard her scold a child. She explained everything patiently and the children drank up her words. She encouraged them to be responsible.

Under Thi's influence, Narén changed noticeably. She took over tasks such as washing, drying, and mending the linen. She also cared for the youngest children like a little mother.

Rats were causing more and more damage to the crops. They attacked everything: gourds, manioc, eggplants, sugarcane—and even the rabbits, ducks, and chickens! Everything went the way of their little teeth, and their numbers were increasing at an alarming rate. A battle against them was waged.

We started by pouring pesticide into the holes. That didn't work, so we moved on to guerrilla tactics. "Guerrilla warfare is always victorious," the party articles said. We dug deep traps. The traps worked, but they yielded only one rat per hole. The others avoided the traps and continued their rampage.

Choeun, the administrator, decided to install an electrical wire around the big sugarcane field. The first night, six rats electrocuted themselves; the second night, just one rat let itself get caught. On another occasion, during the middle of the day, a horse came close to the field and stretched its neck down to graze, the poor animal hurled itself backward, neighing terribly, and then collapsed. The child who was looking after the animal rushed over to it, and then he started to howl. A combatant finally realized what had happened and unplugged the current. The horse was dead and the child was severely wounded.

Ieng Sary, when informed about the incident, limited himself to discoursing at length about the loss of the horse.

Finally, we systematically laid traps every evening, and at the end of a month the rats were gone—from our garden, at least. Meanwhile, people remained concerned that one day rats would spread pestilence or cholera throughout Phnom Penh.

The seminar in July 1978 was organized in a new style. There was a certain pomp that signaled the sprouting of a personality cult. Jeeps were replaced by big, enclosed sedans. It was good form to consider Ieng Sary a hero who had conducted a victorious struggle at the front.

The new seminar hall was equipped with a sound system, a huge stage covered with banners, a map of Cambodia, and a planisphere. Powerful fans beat the air with their big blades, causing a deafening whir—the price of comfort.

Ieng Sary began to speak at once about Cambodia's new system of democracy. "You can't have socialism without democracy," he said. "Democracy is the right and the liberty for each to speak. We have noticed that those directly interested, our peasant brothers and sisters, often don't dare take the floor when it is given to them. And yet, they have something to say. It is in thinking of them that I have formulated a new method of applying democracy. . . ."

Ieng Sary, now silent, assumed an air of mystical inspiration. Everyone held his breath; silence was total.

"To achieve the genuine application of democracy," he continued, "I will designate those who should say what they think. If they refuse to use this right, they will be expelled immediately. Choeun, what do you think?"

"Since the party gives me the right to speak," Choeun said, "I wish to say that the party is grand and luminous, that I am proud to serve it and I pray that it will show me my weaknesses so I can correct them."

And so the movement was launched. All exchanges started in a similar vein. I was solicited, and when I stood up to speak, I concentrated my energy on remembering and repeating everything I had heard.

Next Ieng Sary described the international situation. The American and French imperialists were beneath contempt, of course, and Russia was plunging into an inextricable quagmire, with China following the same path. Vietnam had its back to the wall. Finally, only Democratic Kampuchea—to which all of humanity was turned—offered the image of a powerful nation and a pure revolution.

Evoking the border conflict with Vietnam, Ieng Sary said, "If during their last offensive the Vietnamese troops were able to penetrate so deeply into our territory, it's because they benefited from complicity. Phim, the traitor, the drunk, was their accomplice. The Vietnamese are preparing a new offensive for the next dry season, but we'll break their bones. Now that the region is purged, we have nothing left to worry about. . . ."

"Long live the just and clairvoyant party," people cried, holding up their arms.

"Let us engage in a race with the Vietnamese," the vice prime minister added. "We must first beat the enemy within, and that is done! Now we must build a prosperous country where people live happily. We have already done much, but the traitors have made us lose time. We will now complete the plan—that is, we will modernize transportation in five years, agriculture in ten, and industry in twenty. . . . We will develop leisure and travel. There will be study trips in groups that will permit the exchange of ideas."

The assembly struck up in chorus the slogans written on the banners on the wall.

The party instituted "Socialist movements" inspired by Lenin's "Socialist Saturdays," but better. Work done during these movements was supposed to ensure a unit's self-sufficiency.

We were invited to participate one hour a day after mealtime. Since we were receiving better nourishment, we were told, we no longer needed a rest after eating. This additional task was particularly painful. I had the impression that the party wanted to use us to the limit.

The will to achieve self-sufficiency was implemented in a confused way. How was such a principle to be applied to office supplies, for example? In terms of paper, we could recycle the archives and send them to the factory, but what about the rest?

Using a ballpoint pen was reserved for the old guard. The rest of us had to use pencils, and use them economically. When a pencil became too short, we would attach a pen cap to prolong its life.

Corrections on documents were to be made in ink. When the ink ran low, we added white wine to dilute it—which explained why there was a bottle of white Alsatian wine next to the ink bottle. We inhaled its aroma each time we opened our pen caps!

Eventually we reached the point where we had to dye the ribbons on the machines. In terms of stencils, which I used in quantity, the question was even thornier. There were only a few, and I was expected to type without making mistakes.

When I delivered a stencil, the first thing that was judged was the number of little red marks. One or two marks earned a frown. More than three marks earned criticism. I never submitted a stencil with more than five marks, because whenever that happened, I preferred to throw it out in the kitchen hallway. Obviously, that meant sacrificing the forest for a tree, but what else could I do?

· *Nine* ·

Ieng Sary embarked on another trip to Thailand. For us it meant a colossal amount of work: letters, translations, lectures. I was working on several documents at once, early into the morning. It had become routine to spend two days and a night at a stretch at the office—in fact, leaving any earlier would have been perceived negatively. Amazingly, I was able to keep up the pace. I worked like a machine. My head was empty.

On the last evening, Saê told me that I had been chosen by the party to go on the trip, in connection with the new arrangements to normalize movements within the country. Ieng Sary was taking the train to Thailand the next day, accompanied by several classes of students and two or three wives of recently arrived cadres.

"It is an honor for me to participate in such a trip," I said, asking myself how I could endure any additional source of fatigue.

"You'll have to compose a written account of about two pages," Saê added. "Departure is at seven, they assemble at five."

That night, I sat at the typewriter until 1:30, then went to my room to get some rest. I had just laid down when I heard knocking at the door. I jumped and sat up in bed. Sikoeun jerked me back by my arm. More little knockings followed, until I understood: my daughters! "We wanted to see you! I waited to see the light, then went to look for my sister," Narén said.

It was four in the morning before the girls promised to go to sleep. I resisted the desire to stretch out; I could not miss the departure. At 5:00 I was at the rendezvous, and at 7:00 the train rattled off.

As soon as the countryside started to unfold in front of me, my eyelids became heavy. One of my students came to shake me. "Forbidden to sleep!" she said. I gave a jump. The young girl smiled.

At noon, Ieng Sary invited us to share his meal in his car. What an honor! Roast chicken was on the menu. I had not eaten such tasty meat in years . . . and I could not even lick my fingers!

When the train stopped at Battambang, delegation members stared at me. Of course—I was not supposed to show my face. I mingled with the students while the delegation was received by Ta Mok, a tall, thin, and very alert middle-aged man.

Battambang was even more deserted than Phnom Penh. It was like the vestige of a distant past.

At Sisophon, we were directed, according to rank, toward different accommodations. I shared my space with three other women. In the evening we tried to speak with the cooks, but they had strict orders not to talk to us.

There was no electricity, no lighting. I went to sleep early.

The next morning, Ta Mok proposed taking the women to Samrong. Thrilled, I jumped into the back of the jeep. I wanted so much to see Cambodia!

We started off. I had translated so many articles about the region that I could recite the names of villages, communes, districts, and even the canals that crossed them.

On both sides of the road, fallow rice fields stretched as far as the eye could see. I searched for signs of planting.

Nothing. Only after a dozen kilometers did I see a group of several young women working. Where were the hundreds of people in mobile brigades that the radio had been telling us about all this time?

From place to place, groups of men and women walked around aimlessly, bundles on their shoulders. Looking at their clothes—rags of faded colors, tight pants, torn dresses—one could assume that they were "new."

I was told that new transfers of people had been organized, this mid-year, to correct the imbalance created by the absurd policy of a "band of traitors." In the past, these citizens had been sent to poverty-stricken regions of the Southwest, where, facing utter deprivation, they had had to make a "new conception of the world." The fertile regions were left without labor. In other words, while people starved throughout the country, only a fifth of the planted soils were being cultivated.

Where, then, were the laborers who had worked these fields? Many questions were left unanswered.

And the mobile brigades, so praised for being intrepid at work, lived under very difficult conditions. Meals were brought to the fields: bindweed in boiled water and a bit of rice (about half of what we got in Phnom Penh). With these rations, it was impossible to put forth any real effort to produce. Consequently, the vegetation shriveled and the buffalo stood idle under the sun, looking for morsels to chew.

"The buffalo are fragile," my companion told me. "In the heat, they can't work more than half of the day. And they have to be well fed, given rest, and bathed. . . . In the evening, grasses have to be burned to protect them from mosquitoes. In return, they are able to work under difficult conditions and to labor, for example, in flooded lands. Before, when buffalo were all the peasants had, they were well treated, but now they are almost all dying. And those that survive can no longer work."

I opened my eyes wide. The spectacle was terrible: an indescribable human misery, unbelievable disorganization, a lamentable mess . . .

As the car rolled along swiftly, an old man, waving his arms, seemed to want us to stop. On the edge of the road, a young woman was stretched out, undoubtedly ill. The driver swerved and the old man stayed in the middle of the road, his arms raised to the sky as we passed.

The car finally stopped in front of a big house, where we were obviously expected. A pretty rose-colored drink was served. It was made from a bark syrup. The old cadre gave us specific instructions: "We must organize nurseries and give each child an egg every day. Soybeans must be given up wherever they are not profitable. Around the house, each family must plant sugarcane, . . ."

Then we returned to Sisophon. The train we had arrived on had disappeared, so Ta Mok drove us at high speed to Battambang. The road surface, long abandoned, was in terrible condition.

At Battambang, we rejoined the train and continued haltingly to Pursat, where it suddenly stopped and refused to start up again.

The three women in charge of the trip had everyone step off the train. A large canteen was behind the station, and when Hieng ordered a meal for one hundred people, there was no problem: rice had already been cooked for a team of workers expected later.

During the meal, the train was attached to another locomotive, so we were able to depart (with a crew that looked ill-equipped to me, the daughter of a railroader!).

Back in Phnom Penh, I had trouble recovering from accumulated fatigue. I feared I was a victim of a strange epidemic then ravaging the capital. Neither flu nor dysentery, the symptoms were similar: fever and vomiting. (This epidemic was ultimately attributed to poisoning of the water, and the chairman of the purification plant was eliminated.)

But my sickness was different. It overwhelmed me in waves. Then fatigue melted away in a flow of tenderness. Suddenly, intuition told me I was pregnant. I was seized by the anxiety of an unwanted pregnancy. But how to be sure? I had not menstruated in years, but Sikoeun and I had been together in the spring. I wanted to despair, but a persistent voice told me: This is your son!

I talked to Sikoeun about it and then asked if he was happy. He turned his head, stood up and went to bed without saying a word.

One day, the girls in the kitchen asked me point-blank, "Aunt, how many months pregnant are you?"

I responded at once, hiding nothing. In no time, the news had spread around the unit. People congratulated me. Aunt Phâl's pregnancy was a big event!

In the simple hearts of young combatants, this was good news, and to me, their joy was sweet.

During the second part of the rainy season, foreign delegations kept arriving. Among them was a Swedish friendship delegation led by its president, Marita Huor, a tall, thin twenty-year-old woman with pretty, silky hair.

Marita's husband was Khmer. She had married him during the anti-American war. At the time of liberation, her husband had returned to the country while she was pregnant. Although she had had no news from the father of her child, she refused to believe the news about massacres and even created an association to denounce such stories. She moved heaven and earth to find funding, medicines, and various supplies. Then she organized her expedition.

Upon her arrival, she asked about her husband, for whom she had brought photos of their young son, named Liberty. "We welcome you strictly as president of the friendship association," she was told sharply. "We ask you not to interfere in our affairs. . . ."

Khmers, who are very proud of their independence, said, "She came to spy on us, but we can counteract her!"

The delegation made several visits. The day after the group arrived, an artistic evening was organized in its honor. Right up to the last second, Marita hoped that the authorities, who had welcomed her with such pomp, might bring her news of her husband. It was not to be.

For weeks I didn't have more than three hours of rest per day. Classes, translations, corrections, typing, meetings— it was more than I could handle. Finally, one day when the lunch gong sounded, I didn't have the strength to get up, and I asked Sikoeun to let me rest on the cot in his office. He categorically refused, accusing me of denigrating the good meal that had been prepared. I leaned against the wall, feeling sick. My heart pounded as if it might break. Sikoeun pushed me into the hallway and the courtyard, where I fainted. He went on to lunch, carrying his head high, very happy with himself.

I dragged myself to my room. The distance had never seemed so long. Dizziness swept over me. I thought I would never reach my room.

Sikoeun returned and again took up his diatribe: "You have to be sick to refuse to eat a good meal prepared for you by combatants, our brothers and sisters!"

While husbands were expected to be strict with their

wives, the party was supposed to care for the health of each individual—which is why a jeep was sent to take me in for a medical checkup. All kinds of analyses were made, then the results were lost. The party had a jar of concentrated milk brought to me. As I anticipated the strength that it would give me, Sikoeun demanded, "What have you done to get this milk? The wounded combatants need it more than you. . . ."

Several days before the party's festival, Moch returned. The authorities made it known that she had progressed nicely, which is why she had been assigned to higher functions. The next day and those that ensued, Moch worked on the garden team. She moved happily with the group, a hoe on her shoulder. Showing her joy, she laughed and sang.

Thanks to the righteous line and the patience and warmth of the party, people said, the young depressed woman had been "revolutionized." She had become a party proletarian and the party now called on her for harder tasks. She was proof that members of the former privileged classes could be won over by the revolution.

After a short period at manual labor to "strengthen her links with the masses," Moch came to work at the office. In addition to translating and typing, she was assigned to teach English classes.

Moch took her work to heart, but she encountered opposition among her students, who, used to an Americanized pronunciation, claimed that her accent was no good. They judged her to be incompetent and said it was therefore dangerous to learn from her.

San arrived at this time. The daughter of a large Cambodian family, San had been brought up in China and had lived through the Cultural Revolution. After having

135

brilliantly completed studies to be a pediatrician, she had hoped to marry a Chinese. Chou En-lai made an exception for her.

In 1975, she gave birth to a girl, whom she brought to Cambodia. The Khmer government promised her that her husband would be able to join her on the next plane. But from the moment she arrived in Phnom Penh, the authorities opposed admission for her husband and instructed her to take a Khmer husband.

For months and years, San resisted with all her strength. Criticism, self-criticism, and every other kind of pressure was put on her. Finally, they took away her daughter and San relented.

When she came to B1, San was three months pregnant. The husband chosen for her by the party was far away. The excuse she was given was that he was not reliable.

The activities for the party festival began with the broadcast of revolutionary songs over loudspeakers turned up to full volume. The kitchen team was reinforced to prepare special meals.

The neighborhood movie theater, reopened for the occasion, showed old Albanian and Chinese movies without translation and without correcting the haphazard sequence of reels, but it was enough to excite the public, which forgot all about eating. The meals forgotten, the kitchen girls, led by Choeun, became angry.

The office I worked in was adjacent to Ieng Sary's meeting rooms. Each time dignitaries were summoned to a meeting, a screen was placed in the hall so that I could not see them enter and so that they could not see me. However, one night at the end of October 1978, I arrived at the office just as one of these personalities was brought in by Ieng Sary. He was a large man with graying hair and the calm, confident manner of one who exercises authority: it was Vorn Vet, vice premier in charge of economic policy.

Several days later, I had in my hands an article to translate for use at an official reception. A name was missing among the people present—his. Was it an error? I asked my superior. He was quiet, went to make inquiries, then came back and told me, "He wasn't there." Once again, the Ministry of Foreign Affairs had been the death chamber.

Shortly after that incident, we had a visit from a Chinese delegation. At the last moment, I was asked to type the official speech, specifying that I should not read it. I did just as I was told.

Moments later, Sikoeun anxiously called to me, short of breath, and begged me to retype the speech and take out a paragraph.

As I retyped it, reading it this time, I discovered why there had been a change. The deleted paragraph: "The government of Democratic Kampuchea and the Communist party are certain of being able to count on the aid of the sister Chinese army in case of need."

Sikoeun had to participate in the official reception as the one responsible for the microphones and electricity. I couldn't understand why he had been assigned this task, when he couldn't so much as install a switch.

When he came back, Sikoeun was still trembling and pale. He explained how the electricity had gone out just when the foreign delegation entered the room and how the microphone had gone silent for several minutes during the host's speech.

Sikoeun had let himself be trapped. I sensed that our situation was becoming more precarious and had the feeling we were reaching the end of the journey. I thought about the girls. What would happen to them?

China's refusal to intervene directly was accompanied by the visit of a Chinese army acrobatic troupe that was touring Cambodia. The children attended the performance and commented about it afterward. Narén and Sokha said that a Chinese "aunt" had taken them on her knees and given them candies.

Narén, whose eyes still sparkled with pleasure, showed me how she had grabbed the candies between her hands to distribute to all her friends. "In China, children can eat candies?" she asked me. "Is it richer than here?"

I jumped up and quickly covered her mouth, looking around to make sure no one had heard. Such remarks, adding to her father's frustrations, could only make our position more fragile.

In November, the ministry was reorganized and Sikoeun was put in charge of the press department. I was worried. So far, no one from B1, with the exception of Phon, had survived a promotion. Sikoeun remained indifferent to my concerns. Instead, he was triumphant. He had become deaf to everything I said.

The staff of the Press and Information Department increased considerably. A group of Chinese translators and a Vietnamese section were added.

A group of reeducated people, whose arrival had been promised long before, rejoined B1. Among them were people I had known ten years earlier: Paên, a former student (who had changed greatly); Teary, Chau Séng's nephew; Som, who had lost his wife and four children in the evacuation; Hom, a big, strong boy who had suffered greatly from malnutrition and edemas; and Ti, Joelle's husband, with his new wife.

It was decided that we would move into new offices and were moved to the west wing of the third floor.

We prepared English radio broadcasts first; we would wait to see about broadcasting in other languages. We began by sending telexes in English and French. I composed the dispatches, typed them in capital letters, and gave them to a liaison officer, who took them to a secret place for transmission.

When everything was ready, Ieng Sary bestowed on us the great honor of being received in his office.

"The war of the airwaves is begun!" he burst. Then, after a short introduction, he addressed me: "Phâl, what do you think about the English of the announcers?"

I bit my lip. I did not like this kind of question. His niece Da played a primary role in the English broadcasts. Not only were they unbearably awful, they were incomprehensible. Further, she wouldn't accept a single correction.

Taking a deep breath, I said, "Da has good pronunciation, but Ni does better translations."

Sikoeun shot me a furious glance as Ieng Sary started laughing, as he often did, while looking upward. Not a sound was heard in the room. All participants, no matter what their rank, remained rigid in their seats. It was fairly impressive to see such a grouping of men supposedly in control of a state remain silent, petrified.

"Bad response!" said Ieng Sary. "Da has good pronunciation. Ni translates well. That means nothing."

I was ashamed of this grotesque staging. I longed for the time I had been tending the garden. Even though I had been held in quarantine, I had felt more free.

I repeated what I had just said.

"Yes, yes, I heard you: Da speaks well, she has a good accent. Ni translates better. She also has good pronunciation." Without any transition, he moved to another subject. "When can we start?" he asked Sikoeun.

"December 15!"

"We will start December 1!" Ieng Sary replied. "The war of the airwaves has started; it is your struggle! It is up to you to lead it and win it! On the front, not far from here, the combatants, sons and daughters of our poor but sublime people"—he stopped to cover up a sob—"are spilling their bright red, pure blood for the defense of the home country and our race. They accept the supreme sacrifice. . . . We who are sheltered, well fed, resting under our mosquito nets, would we hesitate to engage in the struggle?"

Everyone was silent and introspective. Ieng Sary spoke for a long time. When he finally stopped, a long silence settled in. People scarcely dared breathe.

"Good," Ieng Sary finally concluded. "Then we'll start on December 1!"

Then he gave instructions. "Sikoeun, will you read us the daily time schedule?"

"Wake-up: 5:00 in the morning. Until 6:00: water the vegetables and the garden and clean the premises. From 6:00 until 7:00: listen to the national radio. At 7:00: salute the flag. From 7:05 until 11:00: main work. From 11:20 to 12:30: socialist movement. From 1:00 P.M. to 4:30: main work. From 4:30 to 6:00: manual work and dinner. At 7:00: take up work again. Ten o'clock: meeting!"

"Bravo!" exclaimed Ieng Sary. "Seventeen-hour days! The superiority of the socialist regime lies in that! We are far from the forty hours per week required by certain revisionist unions. We are far from the unemployment created by capitalism! Here, it isn't work that is missing, it is hands. . . ." He was very happy with himself.

"But beware!" he continued. "You must pay attention to your health! Take care to get rest!"

He was silent again for a long time before concluding on yet another point: "Be vigilant! Among us, there is still a traitor. You must uncover the person! Nostalgia for the Paris life, the French upbringing, life à la française . . . [these are] enough clear indicators!"

At the exit, Sikoeun summoned me briskly. "Who do you think he is talking about?" he demanded.

Drawing the lucky number was to free oneself of all sources of blame that could be brought up later. To deceive oneself was to show complacency and draw suspicions. Saying nothing was considered complicity.

I refused to play this sordid game. According to those he addressed, Ieng Sary let it be known that he was referring to either Keat Chhon or Thiounn Prasith. I kept quiet. Given the uncertain situation in which I found myself, I wanted at least to save face and finish up looking my best, if possible. . . .

The threats became more cruelly specific. Added to maneuverings to place blame on Sikoeun and his poisoned promotion were new elements.

Reeducated cadres who recently returned were presented as reliable people. As such, they were destined to take our place as soon as "the next victory over the Vietnamese" was won. The party announced the arrival at B1 of people who had been convicted of treason and had survived the purges carried out by former elders. The latter had never stopped pursuing those who had managed to escape subsequent purges.

At the end of 1978, I felt a deep weariness and infinite sadness. A sense of freedom had become inaccessible to me. What did it all mean?

Fortunately, this was a period when I could be with my daughters. Since lunchtime had been canceled, I returned to my room only late at night. Then I went to look for the girls under their mosquito nets at the child-care center. We returned, "all four of us," as Narén put it, "little sister, little brother, you, and me." We already loved the little brother-to-come very much.

The first foreign-language broadcasts began at the beginning of December. Officially, the battle was going well, but we knew we were at a turning point. Fighting along the border was increasing. We could not dismiss the possibility that an enemy on the inside or a Vietnamese agent might eliminate Pol Pot and bring a fatal blow to the regime.

The rounds of foreign delegations continued. In mid-December, two Americans and an Englishman came to visit. Malcolm Caldwell was a well-known English academic who wanted to learn more about the Khmer Revolution. The two Americans also clearly demonstrated goodwill. Richard Dudman of the *Saint Louis Post Dispatch* had been imprisoned by the Khmer Rouge in 1970, and Elizabeth Becker had severely criticized the American war in the *Washington Post*.

Initially set for a week, the visit by the three guests was prolonged. Ok Sakun, known as Mén, and Thiounn Prasith, who relieved each other in guiding and accompanying the visitors, began to feel uncomfortable.

As the delegation's visit came to an end, Ieng Sary organized a political seminar. His first speech was very ideological. "All of our acts and all of our thoughts," he explained, "must be dedicated to the nation and the people. One must breathe, eat, and move while thinking about the people, the combatants who are fighting on the front lines. While saluting the flag, you must learn by heart each word of our hymn that was composed by the grand secretary. . . ." Throughout the speech, his bodyguard passed written messages to Ieng Sary.

The second session was cut short. Saturday morning the third session finally took place, and the passing of the written messages resumed. But with the third note, Ieng Sary grabbed his briefcase and left in long bounds, back bent, steps heavy.

The session over, I returned to the office. I had just started working when Sikoeun called me into his office and locked the door behind me. I sat anxiously, fearing some terrible news for us.

Sikoeun also sat down. "They assassinated him!" he said.

Assassinated! The word burned my ears and I felt my strength ebbing away. I didn't think to ask *who* had been assassinated—it could only have been Pol Pot. This meant that a powerful inside enemy was going to impose his law. Blood would flow. We would be arrested and tortured . . . The children! Where were they? We had to go immediately to take them away.

My mind racing, I finally asked him, in a burst of hope, who had been assassinated.

"Caldwell!" he exclaimed.

I was shocked. Why had they murdered Caldwell?

"We must keep the news to ourselves," Sikoeun continued. "You will type the communiqué. Here is the text. No one must learn the news."

After glancing over the first lines, I turned to Sikoeun. "The use of tenses is not correct. Why put the indicative if the guilty person is not known?" I asked, surprised at the error.

"I myself raised the problem with Ieng Sary. The indicative should be used."

"So, we know who is guilty?"

The national radio broadcast ignored the event, but everyone in B1 knew of the assassination. Combatants who had been at the scene told their comrades and their wives everything: the commando had come by a narrow, unguarded street. . . .

· *Ten* ·

At the beginning of the new year, the general atmosphere, reinforced by ideological efforts, seemed optimistic. In fact, the mood at B1 was nearly euphoric. People began to wear colorful clothes, livestock thrived, and the garden yielded more vegetables than ever. Victory was close and the future radiant.

A bomb explosion nearby startled us, but no one was alarmed. "Those are our soldiers training," someone remarked. We continued our work without a clue that a stranglehold was tightening around Phnom Penh.

On January 5, I was awakened by the loud din of the radio. My heart leapt. The subject was incomprehensible, but I recognized the voice as belonging to Pol Pot. I had slept through the wake-up time! Panic-stricken, I got up and walked around the room. I could already hear the critics: a speech from "The Big Chief"—that is something not to be missed! I was angry at Sikoeun for having left without waking me.

Trembling, I adjusted my dress and smoothed my hair, then hesitated . . . Would it be better to say I was sick? I wondered. Finally, unable to stand it any longer, I went out as quickly as my pregnancy—now in its ninth month—allowed me to move. I joined the students who had assembled obediently to listen to the speech.

My heart was pounding and I could not concentrate. It was something about the Vietnamese, but it also had to do with "uniting all of the democratic forces." I did not understand what this meant, since the recent disappearance of the "good cadres" from region number one signified a new wave of purges.

Classes were suspended until new orders were given. I went directly to the office. At eleven, while heading toward the canteen, I was astonished to see that in every direction, trenches had been dug in the soil. Was Phnom Penh going to be threatened? I asked myself. Too tired to think about it, and overcome with hunger, I repeated what I had been told to believe: we will beat the Vietnamese.

All afternoon I translated. I did not leave work until two in the morning. I was quite pleased with myself, as I had caught up on most of the radio bulletins and articles for foreigners living in Phnom Penh.

It was unusual to see lights still on at that early an hour. In the dining hall, people were working feverishly, filling sacks with rice. Confident about the news I had translated all day, I took little notice of these preparations and slept well that night.

January 6 began like every other day. Sitting had become a painful position for me and hunger sapped all of my energy. I felt I couldn't go on, yet I had to. My body cried out for food. I swallowed a big glass of water but it didn't alleviate my hunger. It made me ashamed to be reduced to such hunger—to always be thinking of food. Recently I found myself peeling bananas meant for the rabbits! I was constantly on the lookout for footsteps in the hallway, hoping crazily that it was someone bringing food. Of course, no one ever brought anything.

When the gong sounded to signal the start of the day, I was already well along in my work. Outside, the long lines of unfinished trenches suggested something terrifying. Here and there, groups were preparing salted meat

146

and grilling fish "for the army and for our reserves." "We'll beat the Vietnamese!" people repeated.

My daughters came to announce that they had dug their trenches, then dashed away. I watched them go. In the afternoon, the fever of war preparation reached the offices. Typewriters were packed, along with dictionaries, paper, and pencils. Sacks of rice were distributed in case we would be moved. We were told that "the party, seeking to save all of its forces, may ask you to spend some time in a place that is more safe. . . ."

Then came a dispatch: Sihanouk had just flown to the United Nations. I also learned that my companion at work, sitting across from me just an hour ago, was part of the delegation. People were exulting in the halls: "The party has a just and clairvoyant line. When talking about a union of all democratic forces, the party immediately gives it substance! Sihanouk is a good patriot. Bravo, Sihanouk!"

On my way to dinner, I felt a strange silence—the calm before the storm. I hurried toward the dining hall. It was three-quarters empty! I dropped into a chair. "The children have left by train for Battambang," someone said. "There, they'll be safe and they'll eat well!"

"And you, Aunt Phâl, why didn't you leave with everybody? In your condition. . . ." No one had told me what was going on! I was silent, powerless.

That evening, I settled down once again to an important stack of stencils needing corrections and documents needing to be typed. I attacked the work while thinking about my daughters, wondering where they would spend their first night away. The departures continued. At two-thirty, I went back to my room to rest.

Dawn had not yet broken when I left my room on the morning of January 7. In the cul-de-sac between the buildings and the rest of the ministry, soldiers congregated around crates of new guns, polishing their weapons. There

147

was whispering and the clashing of gun against gun in the gray light of dawn. War was at hand.

At seven o'clock, we reassembled in front of the flag to sing the national anthem in chorus with the radio. We were convinced that the leaders had stayed in Phnom Penh.

When I had put the finishing touches on the stencils, I realized that those in charge of copying them had gone. So much work for nothing! Why hadn't anyone told me? I was dumbfounded and was angry at myself for not having been more discerning. The question was: Why had they wanted me to stay?

We saluted the last convoy, departing under Saê's direction. About a dozen of us stayed behind to ensure that the radio and telex functioned—no small honor!

As best I could, I installed myself in front of my desk and scrawled out translations from the numerous communiqués from the front. All along the Khmer-Vietnamese border, from the extreme northwest (called the "tail of the dragon") to the southwest ("duck's beak"), the Vietnamese were suffering heavy losses. They lost twenty tanks here, ten there, fifty farther on. I kept translating. I was no longer hungry. I thought of my daughters and the child I was carrying. The departures had been explained as a guerrilla tactic to dissuade the Vietnamese from bombing the capital. It was to be a temporary measure of short duration.

I felt sad and alone among these people who turned everything into a state secret. I thought about my family. My children were going to know the horrors of war. If they were lost, how would I find them? Maybe we would not see one another for a long time . . . And what if they were killed? Anxiety gripped me every moment as I tried to work.

Nine-thirty: Hong announced a meeting called by Sikoeun. Once seated, we were informed that we must gather our possessions and be prepared to leave for a safe destination chosen by the party.

I assembled my meager belongings: a dress, a toothbrush ... I thought about how I hadn't had toothpaste or soap in such a long time. I also slipped photos into the bundle, vestiges—more like mirages—from the still-recent past. Several times I had been told to get rid of them, but ... I thought again about the baby. I hadn't had either the time or the opportunity to sew him a little garment. I didn't have a single piece of cloth. I went to the clothing workshop to help myself, but the door was closed.

Before leaving, I tried to bring some order to the office. I carefully closed drawers and cashboxes. I covered the typewriters and even gave things a wipe with a wet sponge so that everything was clean. Then I went back to writing while waiting to leave.

As the evacuation train prepared to depart, people kept arriving by bicycle—from where, no one knew. Phnom Penh was enveloped in a strange atmosphere, already part of a new era.

Ten-thirty: Hong hurried by again. Another session. The group split up into two sections, one that was supposed to eat immediately and prepare to go to Battambang, and another that would eat later and stay in Phnom Penh for now. I was designated to go with the first group; Sikoeun was responsible for the second.

I swallowed the bitter soup. Since morning, the women in the kitchen had made soup using all of the foods they could find that were provisions for the front.

"Rendezvous here in six months," Hong told me, extending his hand.

"Good luck," Sikoeun said to me while shaking my hand. "I'm off to the radio station to pursue our work. The army will protect us." Sikoeun was radiant. His new mission filled him with joy. He had nine people with him, including San.

I climbed into the cabin of the truck, which was already full with two layers of rice sacks upon which eight or ten passengers sat. When the truck started out, I saw Hong give Sikoeun a briefcase. Sikoeun then got into a little van. Hong jumped on his motorbike and left.

B1 was a thing of the past!

"We are going to take aboard the motorbikes and bicycles," the driver said. "They should not be left here for the Vietnamese." The truck also stopped at another unit entrance to pick up tools. It was nearly eleven-thirty when we drove one last time past the buildings of the deserted ministry. The unfinished trenches gave the place a rather strange look—as if an animal had plowed the area with its claws.

Three years before, I had imagined Phnom Penh as very beautiful. I had hoped to make my contribution to the building of a more beautiful and brotherly world.

We reached the banks of the Mekong, where we saw workers walking along in groups. Barges, bulging with their heavy loads, sailed up the river.

"For several days now," my companion said, "the population from the provinces has been moving upriver. The people are temporarily heading for the northern provinces, where they'll be welcomed by the cooperatives."

The truck was about to go under the Chruy Changvar Bridge when someone at the rear cried, "Stop! We left the rice cooking pot behind!"

The driver slowed down and was preparing to turn around when a violent explosion erupted behind us, followed shortly by a second explosion.

"Vietnamese!" the passengers yelled.

"Vietnamese!" echoed the driver, pushing the accelerator to the floor. "They are behind us!" Then he turned to me and asked, "Which way do we take to Battambang?"

At Prek Kdam, the passage between the southern and northern halves of the country, the route was crowded with young, bewildered workers. No possible organizer was anywhere in sight.

The truck moved very slowly. Someone cried that Kampong Chhnang, the first town on the route, had been taken. The driver wanted to turn around. I couldn't believe the situation was already that bad. Still, it was possible. The Vietnamese could have bypassed Phnom Penh before taking Kampong Chhnang.

"We must pass," I told the driver. "Keep going."

The truck got back on the road as fast as it could and we bounced along over the potholes. We remained silent, strained, our breathing suspended and our eyes fixed, on the lookout for the enemy army.

When Kampong Chhnang finally came into view, my heart tightened up at the idea that we might not make it. Would we be stopped? Taken away? And the children—what had happened to them?

We might be executed on the spot! My daughters!—where could they be? I felt like praying.

The truck traversed the deadened town without stopping and we continued onward for a long time. I put my hand on my stomach. The baby hadn't moved in a long time—I assumed he was holding on. If he could just wait until we found his sisters!

At nightfall, the truck reached Pursat and sought out the house for the B1 guests. Three cooks, young women trained at B1, prepared a good cabbage soup with pieces of pork. They made no reference to the current situation, and we didn't whisper a word about why we had arrived unexpectedly. War was raging by now, but it was still supposed to be a state secret!

For the night, everyone except me slept in hammocks. I stretched out in the truck cabin, using my sandals as a pillow. I propped up my legs (and the baby) as best I could.

We continued on to Battambang early in the morning. Having encountered a touring vehicle in the middle of the night, Man-with-the-wooden-leg made me get into the car with his driver. Given my condition, he wanted to limit the risks. I left my bundle in the truck. We eventually reached the Battambang road.

I watched the countryside roll past. No life, no cultivated lands, rice fields fallow for years . . . infinite desolation. Where was the miracle of collectivization? The forces of nature that had been mastered? The happy crowds of believers?

It was obvious that the central power had not been effective in imposing itself. Phnom Penh, the head, had no body, no arms, no legs. Everything had been an illusion and a farce!

As the car reached Battambang, I thought again about my daughters. I imagined being reunited in a quiet place where there was plenty of food. Yesterday's anxieties were already far away. Here, everything seemed peaceful and, above all, inaccessible to the Vietnamese.

I was yielding to these sweet dreams when I noticed a loud noise overhead. Five helicopters circled the town.

"Those are our top leaders," the driver said reassuringly. "They chose to leave Phnom Penh last, to cover the evacuation. Ah, leaders like them, worrying about the security of their people, always ready to sacrifice themselves, there are no others like them in the world, nor in history!"

Moved by this show of confidence, I was half-convinced by what the driver said. But the helicopters had barely disappeared behind a curtain of trees when a group of chase planes burst onto the scene. Three huge explosions went off and columns of smoke rose up.

"Ah, these Vietnamese! They are so arrogant!" the driver raged. "Poipet—let's go to Poipet!"

"No, that is out of the question!" I protested. "You can go, but I am staying! The children are in Battambang, I want to find them!"

We searched the town—but no children. Many people milled about in the station. The bomb explosions had sown the seeds of panic.

The driver went to a gas station—I was astonished that any remained—and then agreed to take me as far as Sisophon. That was the real rallying point, according to what I had heard so far. Apparently, the coconut grove was safer than town. So we sped on to the coconut grove. Once there, the driver suddenly braked, turned off the engine, grabbed his bundle, and slammed the door, saying, "I am going to join the army!"

Before I could even open my mouth, I was alone. My bundle was still in the truck, and God only knew where that was.

It was late, and I had not eaten since the previous day. I walked in circles, searching for a solution. I could take the car and keep going, but that would not bring me to my girls! And where to go? What to do? Call out? Run? Cry? Wait? Wait until the Communist party of Kampuchea, righteous and clairvoyant, deigned to set its sights on the miserable, undesirable, pregnant creature that I was? . . .

I had just determined to keep trying to find the girls when I heard the scratching of tires on the gravel. I hid myself from view . . . and then was surprised to recognize Ny Kân, chief of protocol, getting out of his beautiful car, followed by several young members of his team dressed in ceremonial clothes: white shirt and coat for the boys, white *haul* (a special silk wrap) and blouses for the girls. I walked over to them. Ny Kân was stunned:

"Is that you, Phâl? Phâl of B1?" he demanded. I almost wanted to laugh. He went on: "What are you doing here?"

I recounted events as I had seen them. Everyone gathered around me. Their eyes expressed surprise and doubt. They were all very worried because they had left their things in Phnom Penh.

"And my wife?" Kân asked.

"She prepared your bundle and left it on the table for you to find when you return," I responded.

The young people took turns talking and explained that their mission was to accompany foreign diplomats and technicians residing in Phnom Penh to the border. That was how I learned that the main readers of the documents I had been translating had been gone for more than a month! I wanted to cry at the folly, at the abuse of power. But now everything was over. I was sure of it and felt enormous relief.

Ny Kân stood back several paces. He spoke passionately of the sure and rapid victory over an enemy undermined by difficulties and contradictions. He launched stirring appeals for the survival of the race. He promised reunions in a liberated Phnom Penh and the reconstruction of the country on a new foundation.

"We will win!" he concluded. "Down with the Vietnamese! Up with the party!"

Everyone repeated it in unison.

Late that night, my truck from Phnom Penh arrived. I grabbed my bundle and stretched out under the porch roof of the residence where I had slept on my last trip to the coconut grove. I was neither tired nor hungry. I wanted to be alone to devote all of my thoughts to my girls.

After daybreak, I looked around the coconut grove. I

154

found pretty wooden houses, a well, and a pond in the distant rear. A group of combatants lived there and kept a garden.

At midday, a pot of rice and soybeans was cooked, which we ate with a little salt. There were some provisions available, but we had to be economical.

By nightfall, there was still no news of the children. I searched the alleys and byways. I wanted to believe in Ny Kân, but my anxiety increased with each passing hour. . . .

The following day was equally empty. The young ones, who wanted to join the army, went around in circles like a pent-up herd. Sitting on the floor, I watched the idle crowd. I was also waiting—but for what, I no longer knew.

Suddenly I jumped. Two big black cars jolted onto the scene and each carried one of my children! I ran behind them, but the cars disappeared in a cloud of white dust. The little girls had not seen me. They were huddled in the seats and appeared cheerful. Behind the cars were trucks filled with people—students, cadres, and families—all of whom had left Phnom Penh by train.

Eventually I caught up with the group, which had stopped a few miles down the road. I soon heard an account of their trip, a particularly eventful one. After a long delay in the Phnom Penh station, the train had gotten underway. Later it had stopped several times in open country and everyone had to get off with their luggage.

After the quick departure from the last station, Thi, whose arms were loaded with sugarcane, jars of meat, salted vegetables, and enormous bundles of clothes, had been forced to abandon everything on the road.

Armed men had attacked the convoy.

At Battambang, Thi had wandered about with the whole group before finding the B1 drivers who, in turn, had been combing the area in search of them.

On the walk, Narén had aroused much curiosity. A crowd had gathered around her.

"Who is your mother?" someone had asked.

"Aunt Phâl." she had replied.

"Where is she?"

"She is on the front. She is fighting war on the airwaves!"

I was overjoyed to find my girls! I went to see them in their new house at the southern edge of the grove. I found Narén sleeping on a bench, no doubt exhausted from the long trip. While I watched her sleep, her little sister jumped from behind a bush and, with her charming smile marked by two little dimples, asked me, "Aunt! Do you have something to eat?" Then she slipped her little hand into mine.

At bathing time, the children assembled at the pump. Narén was there and did not hide her surprise, tinged with disappointment, at seeing me. "I thought you were at the front!" she said.

"You know very well that your little brother will soon be born," I told her.

"And Uncle Kong, where is he?" she asked, referring to Sikoeun.

"He said he was going to a safe place where he would be protected by the army. . . ."

"Tell me, Aunt!" Narén was suddenly coaxing. "Are children being taken to the front?"

That night, Narén and Sokha both came to see me, the elder guiding the younger, and wanted to sleep with me.

I was sharing a big, dark room in a house on stilts with forty other women and some nursing mothers. I groped for my bundle and took out a tin can in which I had stuffed some dried bananas handed out by Saê before leaving Phnom Penh. I took one out and cut it into several pieces. My girls sucked one of the pieces and pocketed another.

156

Then they stretched out on the floor and went to sleep. I pressed my lips against their little heads and breathed in their sweet warmth.

Caught in the cross fire of war in a world that was sometimes good, sometimes hostile, we were happy, all three of us—all *four* of us, Narén would say!

I listened to time passing minute by minute.

Saê energetically organized camp life while awaiting our imminent return to Phnom Penh, which everyone was convinced would take place. After a few exchanges, she had galvanized volunteers for the army and inspired even the weakest to help harvest the rice. Within a few hours, she had contacted several cooperatives and divided up the work force. Everyone was settled.

There was still the problem of children who had been separated from their parents. We shared the responsibility. I took care of Soth, the daughter of San, who had stayed in Phnom Penh with Sikoeun's group.

Narén showed me her bundle. All she had taken was a little piece of cloth as a cover. "For Sokha and me," she said.

The next day, it was already late in the morning when Saê called a meeting to assign tasks and divide the work force. While Saê talked, the young people assigned to the cooperatives walked across the coconut grove in closed ranks. I was watching them when powerful rounds of gunfire exploded.

Everyone rose like a shot, grabbed the children and bundles, and left the coconut grove by the south.

I urged on the slow ones while one of the combatants behind us yelled, "Hurry! Go faster! The Vietnamese!"

The gunfire increased in intensity, punctuated by rocket explosions.

Narén and Sokha ran like arrows, but Soth, paralyzed

by fright, refused to move. She cried and asked for her mother. To get her moving I told the child, "Your mother is waiting for you there, under the tree!"

The lie worked once but not twice, and I ended up having to carry this heavy child, even at the risk of precipitating my baby's birth.

People abandoned their possessions in flight. Clothes, kitchen utensils, bags, medicines, sandals, and even guns were scattered on all sides as we ran for our lives.

There were several hundred of us, mostly women and children, moving southward across an open plain. Behind us was a small hill from which the Vietnamese were able to shell us at will.

Upset and worn out by the loads I had given them to carry, Narén and Sokha slowed down, and I caught up to them. Both were trembling with fear; Narén had soiled her underwear without even noticing it. I reached for their bundles and threw them to the ground. The girls began to run at top speed and were soon far ahead of me.

After several kilometers, the word was passed to follow the river. The shrubs that lined the banks would serve as cover for the enemy guns. Unfortunately, concealed among the scrubby trees was wild bamboo, whose needles scratched our faces and dug into the skin of the babies carried in their mothers' arms.

Finally the thicket became impenetrable. To move forward, we had to get into the water. The current was strong and the water, in places, deep; our feet sank into the mud. As a precaution, I took off my sandals.

I had trouble getting back out of the water and later heard that two of the children had tried to gain time by going out to the middle and had drowned.

By the time we reached firm ground again, the fighting had stopped. Or were we too far away to hear? Whatever, we kept on running. A combatant took care of Soth, and I had not given up hope of catching up with my girls when

I noticed a young boy standing ahead of me, looking with large, stunned eyes at the long line of fleeing people. It was Mau, a three year old. Unable to keep up, he had been left behind.

I approached him and he smiled at me. There was no one left behind me, so I picked him up and continued on. Before long, however, I had to resign myself to doing what many others had done: leave my bundle behind. I hesitated for a moment, then leaned over and took back my photos.

I hurried to join a group of girls who had offered to take Mau from my arms. The spot where I had left the bundle was not too far behind, and I thought about going back for it. "Have you seen my girls?" I asked. When they said no, I forgot my bundle and headed off in pursuit of the lead group.

Finally I came to a hollow near the river, where everyone was seated in silence. My daughters were there. They ran over and threw themselves at my legs. Soth was also there, but she stayed seated, looking very sad. I went and took her hand, but she refused to give it to me. Events had so shaken her fierce and independent character. I felt a deep admiration for her, this dedicated little volunteer.

"You know, Aunt," Narén said to me, "we didn't know where you were. We thought you might be lost." She added that she had taken care of her little sister, showing me that she still held Sokha's hand. Sokha snuggled against her sister.

Nearby were two dilapidated straw huts belonging to a couple of ferrymen. They agreed to let us use their barge—an old tub—to cross the river.

· *Eleven* ·

At the height of the opposite river bank, a fairly steep slope, we could see two big columns of black smoke rising above the coconut grove we had just left. In the role of expert, the head of the ministry's political department blamed the mess on the Vietnamese.

How had the Vietnamese arrived so quickly? The effect of surprise was even greater because we thought we were protected and were convinced that our army was inflicting heavy losses all along the border. Was it a matter of a war tactic or were we victims of betrayal? Opinion leaned toward the latter. Son Sen was openly accused, and people said his fate would have been determined long ago except that the party had not wanted to lose his whole network. For good measure, his brother Ny Kân was linked, too, based on grievances against his wife, who was among us.

"Good times are back with us!" people had said. Everyone had believed in the springtime of Phnom Penh. Most of the young women present had a young child or were pregnant, or were just married; their husbands had stayed to defend Phnom Penh.

Ahead of us, a plateau extended as far as the eye could see—not one tree, not one village was visible. "Where are we going?" I asked. I would have liked to be able to understand how and why I should muster the strength to continue. But that, too, was a state secret! It was left to us to stick together and advance.

A long march began. Dry bushes hurt our feet; the crackled, burned, and hardened earth wounded them also. Each step drew cries of pain from the children. As night fell, we lost all visibility, making the march even more painful.

"Get down! Airplanes!" someone cried suddenly. Everyone hit the ground.

Hearing and seeing nothing, I went over to the woman who had sounded the alarm and asked, "Where are the planes?"

"Here, look!" she answered, pointing her finger.

"But those are fireflies!"

Glad that it was only fear that had threatened us, we got up again and followed the unmarked path toward the phantom villages. We were still advancing after midnight, stumbling and faltering more than ever, when in the shadows we made out a grove of trees. Saê advised us to hide quietly while she went to negotiate safe passage. We wondered what need there might be for her to negotiate.

An hour passed before Saê returned. She whispered to us to follow her in silence to the third hamlet: the first two weren't safe.

When we arrived, we found women preparing rice soup. They also opened a container of *prahok*. We drank two big jars of brackish water to staunch our thirst. Several ate from one plate, drinking and lapping up the rice soup. . . . Later, we were grateful to have straw as bedding.

In the morning, I woke up aching and exhausted to a sad and absurd sight. In the middle of the miserable huts, naked children with distended stomachs ran around while women slowly hauled rice, spilling a lot along the way.

The village president strutted about in the middle of the scene and yelled slogans into a loudspeaker to incite people to work: "Let us launch the offensive to harvest the rice!" "Let's concentrate our attacks on the harvest!"

It was understood that we would work for our rice; we were formally forbidden to say that we had come from Phnom Penh. I offered my services on the threshing floor but was told to sit down and invited to sift the rice while blowing on the scattered grains on the ground. My legs felt heavy, blowing made me dizzy, and I soon needed to go back to my bed of straw to rest for a moment before undertaking a visit to the nearby village.

Several dilapidated huts were situated around a big canteen. A few old women were sitting cross-legged under rolled-up mosquito nets which were black with dust. I approached them. They greeted me gladly: "My dear child! What are you doing here, in your condition? In these hard times, what have you come to do in Cambodia?"

"I would so much have liked to bring you something," I said. They gave long sighs.

Mealtime was about to be announced. Men and women, in the proper order, headed toward the river to bathe in two different streams. When the gong sounded the men, the children, and, finally, the women went to eat. There were many people—more than the modest size of the village would have lead one to suspect. Adults and children alike seemed in good health and were fairly well dressed.

Next it was our turn to eat. We put the dishes left by the people before us into a basin of hot water set out for the purpose. (One can imagine the color and smell of the water after hundreds of plates had been soaked in it!) At the same time, the rice was covered by the mosquito nets.

The women working in the kitchen were too few and ill-equipped to do all of the work asked of them. Their only cooking utensils were the small individual jars requisitioned from village families in the name of collectivization. They worked hard from morning until night.

As I left the canteen, several boys in their twenties came up to me. Judging from their clothes, I figured they were city dwellers from the evacuation four years ago. They looked me up and down arrogantly and then assailed me with questions: "Where are you from? How long have you been in Cambodia? What are you doing here? Where is your husband?" Behind me, their older cohorts lay in wait for my answers. The village president came and dispersed them.

I went back to find the old women, trying through them to imagine a mother-in-law I had never met. We talked for a long time. One girl said the harvest promised to be very good compared to recent lean years. People were hoping for an improvement. A little girl showed me a dress and a jacket that the party had just distributed. It was light gray—black was out, apparently, and so much the better.

One of the kitchen women hurriedly passed by. An old woman called to her and spoke warmly about my children. The first woman looked at them, winked, and said, "I will save you some crust of rice. Don't forget to come and see me!"

I was glad to have this human contact. I liked simple people and felt good around them. They had gained great wisdom. The surrounding area was the most beautiful I had seen in Cambodia. Life in this village seemed to pass peacefully according to the seasons, just as it has for millennia.

The next day at lunchtime, just after finding a plate of rice and carefully settling onto a bench to eat, I saw people from my B1 group jump up. Instinctively, I did the same.

"Quickly! Quickly! By the back way!" I heard. I took

my girls by the hand and made a rapid detour to wave at the old women who had been so kind. Once again I was at the rear of a herd in flight.

I was barefoot, which caused me to feel more painfully the sharp stones that were making my feet swell. That very morning, an elder had taken my sandals on the pretext that I no longer needed them. During our last flight, he had discarded his in order to run faster.

A young mother named Huor loaned me her shoes. "What is happening?" I asked her.

"The Vietnamese are arriving by horse. They know that we are hiding in the village. . . ." Lowering her voice, she added, "The village president told his men to attack us to take away our bundles. . . . Some say it is your fault that the Vietnamese know!"

Because of me? Vietnamese on horseback?

We filed along kilometers of dikes, continually pressing to go faster for fear of being discovered. According to the rumors, we were going to Samlaut, an area about eighty kilometers away. It was safe there. We would be there in three, four, or five days.

The word *Samlaut* comes from the adjective *slaut*, which means soft, good. It resonated sweetly in my ears. Samlaut had been one of the first revolutionary bases. The mountains there were full of birds, it was said. In my imagination I was already hearing them sing amid the many-colored flowers. I still hoped to find Sikoeun. If he had not returned from Sisophon, I thought he would certainly be at Samlaut, and I rejoiced at the thought of our reunion.

At the end of the afternoon, we made our way toward a village Saê had contacted about feeding and lodging us. There was talk about a pig being slaughtered for us. . . . We arrived like a herd of donkeys chasing a carrot. Instead of a village, however, we found ourselves in a grange, and instead of a pig, there was nothing at all to eat or drink.

There was only a lake. The water was dirty, but I went

in anyway to bathe and to wash my dress. I was feeling ill. There were a lot of leeches in the lake; in minutes I counted more than twenty attached to my legs.

The barn was crammed when I entered it and lay down along the edge—where I was attacked by ants. I took refuge under the stars but was soon ushered back inside by the same elder who had taken my sandals. For security reasons we had to remain in the barn, ants or no ants. "And if a bomb falls on it?" I said, trying to hide my anger. "What's more, give me back my sandals!"

It was then that a young girl came to tell me she had seen the uncle of my children—Sikoeun—nearby. "I saw him over there, with the other uncles. It was him!" she said with conviction, happy to bring good news. "He carried a gun and smiled at me!"

I felt comforted. The other "uncles" were perhaps the leaders. Falling asleep, I tried to believe that tomorrow everything would be better. But then another piece of news exploded like a bomb: "The Vietnamese have seen us heading toward Samlaut. The radio just announced it. They have launched armored divisions in our pursuit. We can already hear them!"

In a flash, everyone was on his feet. Choeun gave the care of the young children to some capable women and agreed to put me in charge of little Soth. "Sokha and Narén are old enough," she told me. "They should walk alone."

Outside, I saw that a large detachment of the Cambodian army had joined us. There were also several thousand young workers from Phnom Penh. I looked in vain for Sikoeun.

"We are going to walk all night," declared Mén, and we set off in the direction straight ahead of us. Crossing a dried-up swamp, we found it covered with prickly plants. The children's feet became so sore that every step made them moan. They couldn't move as quickly as the combatants, who shoved the children aside in the under-brush and insulted them.

A full moon rose, luminous as a lighthouse, helping us in our difficult march. I looked at the moon to thank it, and it responded with a melancholy smile.

After crossing several kilometers of that unpleasant plain, we reached a dike large enough for a cart to pass. The soil was easier on the feet. Fallow rice fields extended in every direction. Why so many abandoned fields? I wondered. Why had peasants not been able or not wanted to cultivate them?

Without complaining, the children increased their pace. We had just caught up with the others when, next to us, a young woman let herself fall along the side of the dike. She gave a smothered cry, which was followed by the cry of a child: she had just given birth! The doctor was called, but in vain—she was too far ahead. We asked Mén to stop the column. He refused. (Later, he proudly recounted that he thought *I* had given birth.)

A young woman helped the youthful mother, although she didn't know what to do. Two combatants walked back to some trees they had seen that could be used to make a hammock to carry the new mother. Other people hurried on ahead, refusing to see or hear what was happening.

Meanwhile, I had lost sight of my daughters. I ran more than I walked, trying to catch up with them. No one I asked had seen them. I panicked. There were thousands of us that night in the procession on the dike. Elbowing my way forward, I scrutinized the dark, moving crowd. Anxiety mounted with every passing second.

And if my son were suddenly born, like the baby just now? I thought, the panic rising. But I kept on running.

Then I noticed two strange figures resembling big rocks at the bottom of the dike. While curious, I refused to slow down. But then about fifty meters later, without knowing why, I stopped and retraced my steps.

The two somber bodies I had taken for rocks were my daughters. Exhausted, they had sat down to wait for me and had fallen asleep, heads between their knees, indifferent to the passing crowd.

It was no easy task to get them back on their feet. They didn't complain, but they had reached their limit of resistance. On the path again, we once more found ourselves far behind everybody else. But we continued, with no idea where we were going.

In the middle of the night, we rejoined the main body of the group just as people were standing up after a break. I took advantage of the opportunity to suggest to Mén that some combatants help carry my daughters. He looked at me and smiled. Under the brightness of the moon, his smile seemed harsher than the harshest of refusals. He scared me to death. It was one of those moments that only wars and nightmares can create—when the law of the jungle reigns, when friends no longer exist, when the strong crush the weak.

I was thinking about staying at this resting spot until morning, returning to the old women in the village, when someone cried, "The Vietnamese are coming! We can hear their armor!" And so we continued into the black night, the hardest night of my life.

We branched out to the west, cutting across rocky and prickly plains—perhaps formerly rice fields?—then filed along little dikes, tortuous because they were partly caved-in. We stumbled against big rocks, making the march even more painful.

Narén had bloody feet and Sokha was hit by a bout of diarrhea, which completely weakened her. I took turns carrying each of them, but they constantly scolded each other—"A big girl like that being carried by her pregnant mother! Aren't you ashamed?"—and fought to get back down.

Just when I was about to give up, Paên, a boy in Sikoeun's department, took pity and offered to care for Sokha. His kindness was comforting and inspired me to continue.

We reached a canal that was half filled with water. Ignoring the most basic rules of health, no one hesitated to drink this water, swarming as it must have been with bacteria and parasites.

The next region we came to was as humid as the previous one was dry. We crossed many streams, waterways, and little canals where the water was only knee-high. I tried to carry the girls so they would not get wet but ended up stumbling and falling in the chilly water.

At three o'clock in the morning, we reached the edge of a canal at least five meters wide that was blocking our route. It would have been impossible to go back, so we started to cross it, one by one, on foot and then swimming. I sat down to rest a moment and dozed off, then woke with a start. Narén had disappeared. I looked around. Maybe she had left to go to the bathroom?

The moon had disappeared and one could see no farther than one's feet. I gave Sokha to Ri and went to find my daughter, calling her name with all my strength. No answer. Had she crossed without telling me? I went back to where I had left Ri and Sokha. They were gone.

Someone said they had seen Narén leave with an uncle from the army. What to do? I was lost in the middle of this silent moving crowd. I tried to cry out her name, but no sound came from my throat. Was she still on this side of the canal? Was she . . . ? I went into the water, which came up to my chest, and studied the expanse of water. It was black as ink. My God! I implored. Let her be up ahead! Let her not have tried to cross alone!

Once out of the canal, I ran as fast as my long, wet robe would allow. I shivered as much from fear as from the cold. On the narrow bank, it was impossible to walk abreast. To pass on the dike I kept having to go down to the rice field and back up again, risking injury and using more energy.

At four o'clock, I still had not found either of my daughters. Will this nightmare never end? I exclaimed to myself, at the edge of despair.

From deep inside, a voice warned me against the black ideas that always come to assail exhausted minds at the end of the evening. After having spent so many sleepless nights at work, I had learned to recognize them. So I fought off these sirens of despair and called for the minutes to pass more quickly. And I kept on running, descending, climbing.

Just before daybreak, we spilled out onto a swampy plain, where our feet sank in twenty centimeters with every step. There, I finally found my daughters. They were holding hands and walking silently and solemnly.

Our reunion, after so much anxiety, passed in silence. Narén faced me with a pallid expression; her little sister squeezed her hand. None of us had the strength to speak.

Mén appeared suddenly. "Stop!" he insisted.

We were standing between a canal and a steep slope on a passage two to three meters wide, a path of mud so thick that nothing could grow on it.

Exhausted, we allowed ourselves to be stranded in the mud. I took off my sandals to use them as a pillow and stretched out my arm so the girls could lay their heads on it.

When I opened my eyes, not even an hour had passed. The morning light was still weak. It seemed to come from far away. The column had started up the march again, and someone in passing had jostled my wounded legs. I called the girls but they didn't wake up, so I helped them up—I moved my arm and put them on their feet. But they fell over like lumps. Beside them, a young mother and her baby were still in a deep sleep, their cheeks resting on the mud. It was enough to melt one's heart.

Narén and Sokha finally woke up, but once they realized we had to keep going, they turned their faces back to the mud to cry in silence. They refused to get up. This time I could not contain my tears. "I can't go on anymore," I said.

Ri, passing nearby, came and placed her hand under my arm while whispering to me, "Take heart!" Two other women lifted Narén and Sokha, who started wailing. Motivated by some unknown force, I started to move.

We came to something resembling a valley. After several kilometers, when the sun began to drain the water out of our bodies, some people gave up. They said that they no longer wanted to blindly follow the party's orders and that they wished to return to their villages to start a new life.

I no longer knew where I was. I wanted to talk to Sikoeun. He couldn't be far, since he had been seen yesterday. I couldn't understand this situation—I, who only a few nights ago was translating articles singing about victory. I only knew that I had been bypassed by events and that I was exhausted. My thoughts swirled around in my head. I walked like an automaton.

As we left the small valley and entered a vast plain covered with tall shrubs, one message swept through the column: "After the second clump of trees is a village. We'll stop and make something to eat there."

As far as I could see, there were no clumps of trees. But with the prospect of a meal, everyone went as fast as possible in order not to be abandoned. We walked in little groups, strung out for kilometers, hidden by tall grass. At every fork, the direction to take was marked by a broken branch or trampled grass.

The first clump of trees finally appeared at two in the afternoon, and we did not reach the village until four. Those who arrived first had already settled in, some in the shade of stunted trees, others in front of the huts. Not a soul lived in the village—only a dozen or so puny, crazed chickens racing in every direction. The huts were empty. The threshing floor seemed to have been abandoned suddenly, in the middle of a job. The silos were already half full with the new harvest. Obviously, the inhabitants had fled. To escape the Vietnamese?

We pounded rice in order to cook it, without touching the reserves. Being used to the life of harvesting gave us a big advantage. For example, Sin managed to make an excellent soup with herbs found at hand. Some caught small fish in the lake with their hands, others shot sparrows. They were meager catches, yet they made a feast.

Paên found a seed that gave off a sweet taste in water. He filled a gourd with it and gave it to the little girls. Everyone tended their different chores and chattered at ease.

But for me, everything had taken on a whole new dimension. I felt incapable of living this kind of life. I couldn't come to terms with myself, nor could I count on others: everyone was so tired of his own fate!

In this little village, which I would never have been able to find on a map, separated from the world by kilometers of fallow land, rocks, and marsh, lost in the desert and deserted, I had crossed the point of no return. Yet, I had no choice but to go on.

Narén and Sokha slept on the ground. I shifted to give them a little shade. It was painful to look at their feet. Their clothes were shredded and covered with mud, and

172

their eyes were big, sunken circles above their pale cheeks.

Nevertheless, I was immensely happy that we were together.

Just before nightfall, the order was given to leave. No one asked why, as this deserted village hardly inspired confidence.

We reached a plain covered with elephant grass that was taller than we were, then crossed a small wooded area before spilling onto another plain.

It was pitch dark, and we kept stumbling on rocks and in holes. I fell several times. By now my legs were so swollen, so heavy, that they no longer had any feeling or reflexes. Narén automatically took it upon herself to walk in front of me and patiently point out all of the pitfalls. Paên and Hom, since they carried the cumbersome kitchen things, decided to stay near me, too. With so much support, I felt like I had wings.

The moon finally rose softly behind the trekkers. Huge and red like a setting sun, it embraced the wood with a purple halo.

Panic again swept through the column of people as someone screamed, "Fire! Fire! They lit a fire!" But soon the moon was bathing the earth with light. We continued walking across the plains and through the woods.

When we reached a stack of dry grass, it was decided this was where we should spend the night. The best informed stretched out toward the west, the side thought to be the hottest at night and least humid at dawn.

I gathered some dry grass to spread on the ground and to cover us. But the grass was unbearable, as it scratched and cut our skin. The girls, one after the other, had diarrhea. Just when sleep was about to end our miseries, the rosy dawn started to appear and we began shivering from the cold.

We broke camp early to walk until the sun was at its zenith. After just enough time to cook rice bouillon and eat it, we were on our way again. No one would tell us where we were going. From time to time, one or the other elder appeared briefly, but secrecy prevented them from answering our questions.

Eating rice bouillon raised serious problems, because there weren't enough plates and spoons, and those who had not abandoned these precious utensils did not like to lend them.

One generous soul gave us the hollow cover of a mess kit. I had to wait in line to have it filled with bouillon, then I quickly took it to Narén, Sokha, and Soth. The bouillon was too hot, and when it was finally drinkable, the pot was empty! For hundreds of us there were only a couple of pots. When the signal to leave was given, the girls had managed to drink a few gulps. I had had none.

We walked late into the night, taking advantage of the bright moon and freshness of the air. We started up again early the next morning, until noon, when the sun got so hot that the soil burned our feet—and also when the reconnaissance planes appeared. We used that time to have our one meal of the day before heading out—straight ahead—without encountering a village or a soul.

The strongest of our group, the ones who were able to carry the sacks, ate rice. The others had only bouillon or water. The difference might seem minimal, but in fact, it marked the boundary between life and death. For those at the top of the ladder, this march was an adventure. Those at the bottom had to keep pushing back their limits of total exhaustion.

* * *

One night, we arrived in a village made up of a row of nice huts, most of them recently built. They were large and clean. Backed against the forest, they faced a huge clearing where a volleyball court had been installed in addition to a carefully kept garden of varied plants which did not seem to have suffered from the heat.

Several jetties jutted out into a pool. Farther on was a half-full silo of rice that was well protected against rats. And in a shelter that served as a kitchen there were two cauldrons (like those we used in Phnom Penh) filled with rice.

This little corner of life, organized in the forest in the middle of nowhere, was surprising in more ways than one. It could not have been a peasant community—it wasn't their style. Nor was it a mobile brigade—there weren't enough fields surrounding the place.

So the question was asked once more: Were the inhabitants fleeing the Vietnamese, as the leaders said, or were they fleeing from us?

We cared for the vegetables, cooked the rice, and fashioned spoons from wood. The fortunate owner of a plate could even have soup. Then we cleaned up. In the space of a day, we renewed our strength.

Several peasants joined us. They presented themselves as innocent peasants pursued by the Vietnamese. Mén accepted them.

Choeun was in charge of a group of "guests" whose presence was supposed to be shrouded in secrecy. We were not to try to go near them.

At the end of the afternoon, Hong joined us. (How did he know where we were?) He burst out laughing and asked what had made us leave the grange so suddenly. "Saê had searched nearby for hospitable villages," he told us. "When she came back, no one was left! You had flown off like a flight of sparrows. There was never an alert of Vietnamese armored divisions. . . ." Then he added, "I have good news: tomorrow, we are going back to the coconut grove."

Everyone was thrilled at the prospect of finding his or her bundle and recovering a dress, a shirt, a knife, a can of milk, sugar. The discussions lasted late into the night, and in the excitement an extra cauldron of rice was boiled. We had to celebrate the good news!

That the story of enemy forces at our heels on the dike was a cruel machination, I did not doubt, but this story about going back to Sisophon seemed incredible.

The enthusiasm lasted but a moment, like a lull during a nightmare. We had just gone to bed—it was two in the morning—when Hong came to me and whispered, "The Vietnamese are arriving! We have to leave immediately by the forest."

Quickly and silently, everyone left, following a path through the forest that had to be cleared by machete. This was a tedious process and we were all backed up, waiting for the passage to open. If the Vietnamese had found us, they could have taken us like rats in a rat hole.

By daybreak we had gotten only a few kilometers from the village, moving ahead step by agonizing step.

Our path was to the west. For those with any notion of direction, it became clear that we were no longer heading for Samlaut but rather toward the Thai border.

Since we had denigrated our Thai neighbors behind their backs, the situation would really have to be bad before we would consider taking refuge in Thailand! And in our wanderings through the countryside, we came to realize that we were fleeing with peasants who we had put to flight!

As the days and challenges multiplied, I realized that in

the language of the Khmer Rouge, "total control of the country" meant administering a capital emptied of its population, and "the unanimous support of the people" was satisfied by gathering around oneself a few dubious and expedient leaders. The so-called miraculous harvests could be counted on one hand. The happiness of the people remained a pious wish and the cultivated gardens a beautiful fantasy.

· Twelve ·

Now I was glad to be headed for Thailand. I started to sing to help the girls along. The sun seemed less severe, the route less difficult, our feet less painful.

All three of us walked at the same rate, united in one song celebrating a fresh, wonderful world covered with gardens, criss-crossed by canals, and inhabited by people with pure hearts.

That day, during the midday break, we pushed on until we found water. We ran into the wives of Khieu Samphan and Hong, who had given birth two and four days, respectively, before the evacuation. They had been moved by cart (which proved that there *were* other methods of travel than those we had taken!).

On the lake's edge were the shells of large mussels. These served wonderfully as spoons. Life was organized by small groups in an effort to better divide up the food. Narén, Sokha, and Soth now had several grains of rice in their bouillon, and I got my first taste of rice in two full days.

The girls, with their all-serious faces, told me things they heard here and there. That is how I learned that "secret uncles" were concealed in a grove of trees. Still convinced that Sikoeun was among them, I started walking toward the trees. The place was strictly guarded and, to discourage me from getting closer, Choeun offered me a large ball of white rice that had been wrapped neatly in a handkerchief. It went down easily!

I was told that no one had seen Sikoeun. They knew nothing about him, they said, not even whether he had been able to leave Phnom Penh.

I went back to the girls. The signal to leave was about to be given when suddenly, from the other side of the path, a submachine gun opened fire. I stretched out on top of my children to protect their heads, while at the same time trying to be careful about the baby I was carrying. This is it! I thought. We were surrounded during this long stop and there is no escape. We're all going to die.

The gunfire increased. Panicked, Sokha got away from me and ran into the brush. All around her the bullets sprayed—into the ground, under her feet, and between her legs—making the dirt fly. Taking advantage of my shock, Narén and Soth also fled, fast as lightning. I got up and took off after them. I quickly caught up with them, because facing us was an impenetrable wall of wild bamboo. "That way!" I yelled, pointing.

A bit farther on, we encountered another bamboo wall. By now the gunfire had stopped. Straining my ears, I didn't dare move. Silence. Without stirring, Sokha, pale and still trembling, lifted her eyes toward me and pleaded, "Can I go to the bathroom?"

We didn't go back to the site, where people were already questioning witnesses. Instead, seeing Choeun gliding through the trees followed by his "guests," I took my girls by the hand and we mixed in with the crowd to escape the roadblocks, searches, interrogations, and other hassles that would no doubt ensue.

A roadblock had already been set up. We went with the

cooks at the back of the line, in order to not see whatever it was that was not to be seen. A combatant put me on guard: the soldiers who began the march would impose a fixed pace. I reassured him and he let us pass.

The cooks already knew a lot about what had just happened. One person was dead and three were seriously wounded. The peasants, who had been considered loyal, had taken advantage of a combatant's fatigue by grabbing his rifle and firing it at point-blank range.

One of them was stopped and immediately executed, another escaped.

We filed down the road at a hunter's pace, constantly repeating the orders given from the top: "The sides of the road are mined, walk in the middle, absolute prohibition on relieving oneself!"

Ears numbed by gunfire, hearts aflutter, we continued, our thoughts concentrated on the path zig-zagging between mines, when suddenly, BOOM! Everyone froze in place. I grabbed the children to keep them from running toward the side of the road. Then bursts of laughter erupted from the back of the column. I laughed, too, when I saw the cause of our fright: between two cooks, the branch holding the big pot of rice had broken and the pot had fallen, echoing like a mine but without spilling!

No one slowed down. It was getting late; the night would soon envelop us and make progress more dangerous. The pace quickened. Children followed without a word. As we left the forest, the moon illuminated the plain. We went into some tall shrubs. Under our feet, we felt the furrows of an old plowed field—another field abandoned long ago.

Each one stretched out, trying to wedge himself between the hard clumps of earth.

With the first arrivals from the rest of the unit, we learned that in addition to the one who died at the site, three of the wounded had died. Hom was a good person from the peasantry, simple, honest, and hardworking. Ra had been one of our best students of English typing. He was serious and intelligent and excelled in everything. I also knew and thought highly of Yoeun and Him. They both had the sad expression of poor peasant children, but they knew how to be happy and liked to tell funny stories.

They were all between nineteen and twenty-two years old.

That night, I couldn't sleep. Death was too close. It had just taken four young people today. Who would it take tomorrow? I saw myself as a leaf being carried away by the current, with no control over my destiny.

The next morning, a national broadcast picked up on a transistor spoke of various victories. I hoped, in vain, to hear a broadcast in a foreign language. What had become of those who had stayed to carry the torch of "the war of the airwaves"? I thought I might be a widow, that my child would never know his father.

As usual, the radio broadcast the national anthem. We might have taken it up in chorus for those who had died the previous day, but instead, everyone was silent. The possibility of the enemy around us was paralyzing.

We took up the march going west-by-northwest. The young people were still in front, followed by the long procession of women carrying their children. I usually stayed carefully in line, walking with my daughters. The line stretched for several kilometers. Directions were passed down by word of mouth. They were unspecific: after the clump of bamboo, cross the plain, leave the path at the third bend on the right, and keep straight toward the west, passing above the fence. . . .

These directions inevitably became jumbled as they were transmitted down the line, and we were steered toward randomly chosen paths. Amazingly, we found our way every time.

As we approached the mountain range, conditions worsened. Water was scarce. We might go a whole day under the torrid sun without eating or drinking. The coolness of night would briefly allay our thirst, but then the next day, the sun's heat would seem to intensify. Our only defense was our determination to hold on—to hold on at any price. Thus we advanced, lurching on the narrow, tortuous embankments. The children showed extraordinary courage. They fought their battle silently. Finally, at noon, the girls complained for the first time about shadows passing like trees in front of their eyes.

It wasn't until the end of the second day that we realized that the air had become charged with moisture and freshness. We took heart. At the end of the path were recently replanted rice fields and a reservoir of water. Seeing patches of soft green lifted our spirits and relieved our fatigue. Our meal was water!

We no longer could count the days since we had last washed.

That night, Man-with-the-wooden-leg joined us on a cart pulled by buffalo. He promised a distribution of rice for the next day, but added that we would have to undertake a stretch of two or maybe three days without food or water.

The first to see the cart bringing the rice ran toward it, crossing a steep ravine on a narrow tree trunk. I arrived too late.

My daughters suffered incredibly. Their legs could no longer support them. They wanted to cry while walking, but didn't have the strength even for that. And the greater the pain, the harder the effort. They no longer wanted to listen to me.

"If we keep up this pace, we still won't be there in five days!" railed the leader.

The next morning, which was to be the last day of this long march, the girls refused to budge. I coaxed them, but to no avail. Everyone else had left, and I started to panic. No one had even offered to hold the girls' hands, much less to carry them.

I was in a state of despair when Ri, who had stayed behind to look for some medicinal plants, came to our rescue. She generously pulled a packet of sugar out of her bundle and offered a spoonful to each child. They savored it for a long time, then, without a word, got up.

The sun had overpowered us again when we encountered some young people from a mobile brigade who were carrying water. "There is a dam five kilometers behind us," they explained, which said nothing about why they were taking the water so far. They kindly offered us some. To me, they were the incarnation of Providence.

Those five kilometers turned into maybe ten. We walked a long time before reaching the Revolution Dam. But along the way we had the pleasure of rejoining the human race. We met people who had evacuated Nimit, a little village just off Route 5. They had rushed to harvest the rice and put it in a safe place before the advance of the Vietnamese. Their beautiful harvest had been unequaled in this area.

The dam held back a vast pool of water where buffalo bathed. Groups of people talked along the edge. I felt like I was just returning to earth after a long voyage to hell.

Then a truck sent by Ny Kân took us to Mâk Hoeun, his headquarters. There was a crowd of people. Several teams of women prepared food for the army from morning until night. Kân gave instructions that everyone would be able to eat to his heart's content—on plates and with spoons! We were also able to bathe, and a nearby sugarcane plantation was open to all.

On a military map, Ny Kân showed us the route we had taken. "As the crow flies, you covered one hundred and twenty kilometers," he said. "In reality, you must have done double that," he added, tracing his finger in a zig-zag.

I heaved a sigh of relief. Now I would be able to give birth in peace. For twenty-three days and twenty-three nights I had covered hills and valleys, under the torrid sun and in the freezing nights, past gunfire, between mines. All I had left was a sad collection of photos and happiness in knowing we were safe and no longer had to fear the worst for the baby. That night we slept in a hut —a real comfort, even if mice and rats, disturbed by our presence, ran over our legs and arms.

Kân decided to keep the young people with him, so that they could serve in some capacity in the army, and to send the women, the babies, and the young students to Boeng Béng, in Phnom Malay. This part of the trip was made by truck.

Boeng Béng was a rear-base camp used by Thai Communist party guerrillas. At the entrance they had built a kitchen, shelters, dormitories, and a hangar. Farther back from the road was a hospital, a new kitchen, and another dormitory. A big pond had been dug. Tobacco was growing between the trees. Chickens, a rooster, and two pigs roamed near the hospital, and a couple of dogs ran around. A lot of snake skins were stored in one of the shelters.

Our group stayed in the hospital, which seemed to have been evacuated recently. I chose shelter under a mahogany tree. Between two roots I spread some grass out for the girls and me. The ground was flat and the space just our size.

Life quickly became organized. We put all of the children without parents, including Soth, under the care of several young women. Water supplies were rationed, as was the duty roster for the kitchen and for the night watch against tigers and other predators. Yôm and his wife Sim, an older artisan couple who had come to B1 several months before the recent evacuation, were experts in traditional medicine and explored places where they might find medicinal bark, leaves, and roots.

All of the women and girls rejoiced that my baby had withstood the many tests. Many of them, searching the bottoms of their bundles, took out bits of cloth, a needle, and thread. I could quickly sew some little clothes.

Under the porch roof which served as the kitchen, we quickly set up a raised bunk which, according to custom, was used for births. We expected to be spending some time there, as most of the women were pregnant.

Despite the dysentery, which sapped my energy night after night, I awaited the event with calmness. One night, thunder rumbled all around us. It was the first since we left Phnom Penh, and it took us by surprise. Those settled in the hospital weren't bothered; my daughters and I found refuge under the kitchen's porch roof. Unfortunately, it leaked. Our only recourse was to sit on our clothes to keep them dry until the rain stopped.

The next day, Cheat, who headed our group, decided to extend the porch roof. I had my first labor pains that night. Given the intensity of the contractions and the strain of the march, I figured the baby would not be slow in coming. Nevertheless, I decided to wait until the last moment to alert the others. I was happy to be alone to fight through the night. The pangs kept coming. The rooster cried a first time, then a second. I wanted to wait longer.

When the rooster cried the third time and the women came to light the fire to cook bouillon for their babies, I was still waiting. Ying, the doctor, looked at me and understood. She leapt up as I tried to run to reach the bunk. Within a minute, a curtain was hung up around me. The

186

midwife, a nineteen-year-old woman, came with a gas lamp and the child arrived.

My son weighed no less than three kilograms. His first reflex was to suck my heel! Narén, who had lifted a corner of the curtain and watched the birth, exclaimed, "Isn't he cute."

The doctor and midwife offered help to the extent that their training and customs allowed—notably, to expel the placenta and to massage and pound the stomach in a very brisk manner. I had torn, but since there was nothing to be sewn up with, it was left to time to do the healing.

The child really was beautiful. His bare forehead gave him an air of wisdom. His pretty ebony-colored hair covered the back of his neck. He had big eyes and a delicate mouth. In his sleep, he smiled often and even laughed.

News of the birth spread quickly and many came to visit. Everyone agreed he was beautiful. People suggested names. I decided to call him Béng, for the name of his birthplace and the tree that grows in such large numbers there: a tree that is strong and straight, the mahogany. "My son will be strong and straight, his spirit and his heart pure and precious like the mahogany," I said aloud.

It was February 17, 1979.

From Mâk Hoeun, Kân sent a special load of supplies that included meat, rice, vegetables, sugar, and coconuts. A good meal was prepared for me and cloth was found to make diapers. Warm water was brought so that I could wash up. For their part, Yôm and his wife scoured the mountainside all day to find three items indispensable to a good concoction of theirs: a "grateful" vine, bark from the "fire tree," and a certain root that is almost rare in this region. To spare me any effort, they took my clothes and those of the children and washed them twice a day at a border stream more than five kilometers away.

187

Beyond the joy of having a son and of being warmly cared for, I once more began to see the specter of death: my milk would not come! How would the child survive?

Nursing mothers offered their services every time the baby cried. Concoctions were prepared that were so acrid they made me scream when I drank them. Sim gave me traditional massage. All of these efforts finally paid off: I began to produce milk.

Béng was a sweet baby. He looked like an angel brought from heaven. I never tired of gazing at him. I told him that I loved him, and Narén enveloped him with tenderness. She took care of the soiled diapers, saying, "I like to wash little Béng's diapers."

Eight days after the birth, we heard foreign news for the first time. That is how we learned that the People's Republic of Kampuchea had been proclaimed in Phnom Penh after our departure.

"And Sikoeun?" I asked.

"He just joined us at a base not far from here. The group is complete."

Then, very quickly, conditions at Boeng Béng worsened to the point of being precarious. Rice was lacking and the pool of water dried up. We had no more salt and, in this age-old forest, there was nothing left to eat. For ten kilometers around, there wasn't a single vegetable, root of manioc, or yam. Angkar, as we again called the leadership, sent us a pair of buffalo to get water from the stream and supplied us with a bit of salt. We also received a strict warning: as a rear base, we could not claim supplies. Rather, we were to contribute toward supplying the army.

We explored every possibility. We could have cleared a stretch of forest but didn't have any tools. To clear land, the women had to use fire.

We searched the stream bed and found three dozen

shells which somehow would have to be shared among more than 150 hungry mouths. We ate leaves, but this carried its own danger because cases of poisoning had been reported. Driven by gnawing hunger, we gratefully consumed everything that was edible. One day we caught a puppy and roasted it for dinner—a true feast. The other puppies, the mother, and then the big dog were next.

Every night, we heard cannons blasting. Our situation was difficult, but we didn't feel we had the right to complain. "Once we have taken Nimit," Hong said, "we'll go and live well there."

In all of the broadcasts I had translated, I had never heard of Nimit—meaning it could not have been an important village, much less a strategic point. Then why didn't the army take it more quickly? What exactly was happening? Having just come from the front, Sin assured us that the outpost would fall within five days. A little later, Saê gave it eight days. But the nights passed, lulled by cannon fire, and Nimit did not fall.

The heat of the dry season increased daily. The buffalo, also undernourished, were easily exhausted and soon only made their rounds once a day. One morning, one of them left the path to graze and stepped on a mine. That marked a huge loss, because the contribution of meat could not compensate for the loss in water supply.

That night, a truck arrived. Everyone rushed to meet it, our sole link with the outside world. In addition to news, it often brought supplies. Unfortunately, this time it brought only a bit of elephant meat and green *jaques*—jackfruit—and it took away the remains of the buffalo!

We had to recognize that our group did not succeed in providing for its own needs and that the domestic situation was getting worse. Two children died after being brought to a rural dispensary. Cases of dysentery multiplied, whooping cough spread, and an epidemic of scarlet fever broke out. There was one miscarriage. Every day Yôm and

189

Sim covered dozens of kilometers, at the risk of stepping on mines, to find curative bark or roots, but the Phnom Malay Forest was a poor source of medicinal plants, or it sheltered ones that were very different from those they regularly used.

It was decided by Angkar to send women with babies over twelve months and women who were less than six months pregnant and thus could work to a cooperative in Sala Krao (in the south), and to gather the others together in Pailin, one hundred kilometers from Boeng Béng.

Departures took place over several days. They were worried about moving me, so I waited until the last trip.

Although I normally had a high resistance to disease, I finally succumbed to malaria. On the eve of my departure, I had my first attack. All afternoon, semidelirious, I asked to see Sikoeun, since he wasn't far away. I wanted to be with him.

I could no longer stand this life-style. I couldn't take care of myself, which made me too much of a burden to the community. It was time to find a solution.

The doctor and person in charge assured me that in Pailin they would do whatever was necessary for me to see the top authorities. In addition, Huor, who had so kindly loaned me her sandals, stayed near me to feed my son with her milk.

It took a day's journey by truck to reach Pailin. The condition of the roads was horrendous. Every minute or so, the truck would hit a hole that would send its passengers flying in the air and onto one another. Tree branches struck our backs and faces and bamboo pulled at our clothes. Over and over, the truck ventured up steep slopes and crossed precarious bridges made of tree trunks. That was notably the case at a place called "the Frenchman's Falls." The ordeal seemed endless.

Reaching Pailin that night, I was delirious again. The

190

doctor stayed with me and Voeun, the new person in charge, did not leave my side. When I recovered the following evening, many people stood around my bed. Voeun had been very afraid that the fever would be fatal. She had sent a messenger to Sikoeun to warn him of the danger and to ask him to come immediately to my bedside.

Sikoeun made a pretext of having work of the highest importance. I was neither surprised nor hurt. I drew enormous comfort from Voeun's concern and that of other companions. They found canned milk for me and baked goods with crushed manioc and coconut. Each one offered me his ration of meat. Their generosity and solidarity in distress were touching.

At Pailin, we had the privileges of water at our doorstep and of sleeping in a stone house, but the distance was even greater and getting supplies was even more difficult than at Boeng Béng. We soon used up the pieces of manioc and green bananas left over from the huge fires that had ravaged everything. Thereafter, our food supply consisted mainly of red ants and acidic green mangoes.

The baby was fed a bit of rice bouillon. I had no baby bottle and had to put it into his tiny mouth with a big spoon. The poor child was given warm bouillon only once a day. The rest of the time, cold bouillon had to suffice.

The region was infested with anopheles mosquitoes, and both of my daughters had high fevers. Six months earlier, the radio had announced that malaria had been wiped out in 99 percent of the country and that the Pailin region was 98 percent malaria-free! What evil schemes had I been an accomplice to? The whole Khmer reality was so very different from what we had fervently believed!

Not a dozen days had passed before the terrible problem of supplies was joined by the threat of attack.

One morning, refugees flooded Pailin. Some came from

the province of Takeo, others from Kampong Som. They were in their fourth year of wandering around the country. According to them, the "White Khmer" (counterrevolutionaries) were going to attack. In the early afternoon, the threat materialized. At four o'clock, orders were given to prepare to leave at dusk. Vietnamese troops were a dozen kilometers away, people said. We would have to leave the village quickly, at nightfall, and find refuge in the forest.

Just the thought of a long march left me exhausted. The moon having risen, we were supposed to delay our departure. We gladly waited. Two trucks came for us. One carried the famous "guests" and everyone else crammed into the second along with their bundles. Fortunately, one of the people in charge invited my two girls and me to sit in the first truck's cabin.

As usual, we were not informed about our destination. But when, at the break of dawn, we recognized Sala Krao, we understood that we were going back to Boeng Béng.

At Sala Krao, those we recognized from B1 were completely unaware of the Vietnamese offensive. A truck came the next day to take part of the group, and the others fled, barely escaping a hail of gunfire.

In a period of several days, Boeng Béng had changed. Fire, perhaps from our clearing efforts, had ravaged at least five hectares of forest. It slowly continued to consume huge hundred-year-old trees. The scene was spectacular.

The first person I ran into was Ri. Dedicated as ever, she went to get me some water lightly flavored by coffee. She was astonished to see us back at the camp. According to the news she had heard, the situation was excellent. She had even been preparing to reorganize the language classes that had stopped three months earlier in Phnom Penh.

Once again we settled into the old hospital, knowing full well that it was a temporary solution, since it was already clear that we could not be self-sufficient. Near us, a big tree that was smoldering threatened to fall on our dry grass roof. We tried without success to render it harmless; when night came, we set up a guard and then went to sleep under the ball of fire. A providential and unexpected rain fell (at the end of this dry season), soaking us as well as extinguishing the fire.

Three minutes later, a baby kicked over a kerosene lamp and the hut was enveloped in fire.

The next night, the guards were taken by surprise by strange lights accompanied by equally strange birdcalls. Anxiety kept us awake, seated, eyes scrutinizing the darkness.

It was clearly impossible to survive in this place. Ny Kân, who had come to appraise the situation himself, organized another evacuation and dispersal of women into area cooperatives. It was a temporary solution, obviously, because it wasn't good for us to be dispersed.

I was taken to a resistance hideout deep in the forest, where I was sure to receive at least the minimum food needs and care for the baby.

This unit's regulations were very strict, for what in this case were clear security reasons. There were only a dozen of us, including Mân and Ri. One thing we had to be careful about was that the children didn't cry. The clearing was limited to a small space so that we were not visible to reconnaissance planes. We were far from prying eyes, but equally far from any source of water—the border stream was more than an hour's march away. People went there in rotations, one day in five, to bathe and wash clothes.

I was given a toothbrush. What a pleasure it was to brush my teeth again!

It was hard for me to stay put from morning until night with the crushing heat of the end of the dry season, and then from night until morning, giving my baby a dry teat to suck, in order to keep him from crying. But life was fairly pleasant. My daughters recovered and the baby grew. Everyone showered him with tenderness and compliments.

· *Thirteen* ·

We spent only twelve days in this peaceful little haven. Announcement of an imminent Vietnamese offensive put us back on the road.

I carried little Béng in a scarf, as do the Cambodians.

He tried to smile, producing two beautiful dimples. The girls each carried a little bundle and walked in the terrible heat without complaint. We picked up and followed a border route. At nightfall, we halted and were joined by other groups. I recognized the Thiounn Thioum family, an aristocratic family that had joined the revolution, and moved in next to them.

Along the edges of the path, we heard neither cannons nor rockets. Instead, from the other side of the border came the sound of motorbikes and cars. The traditional New Year was approaching and at night we let ourselves be rocked by the rhythmic songs accompanied by drumming that punctuated the festivities.

On one side of the border, people fought, blood flowed, the dead were counted. On the other, people sang, danced, laughed. . . .

Everyone knew we couldn't stay, but it was decided to build a shelter and to outfit it with beds arranged in dormitory style. The tremendous monsoon rains were not long off.

We still hoped that, once the offensive passed, we could return to where we had come from.

That night, the sky was covered. I prepared my mat of grass and leaves, just before sundown, at the precise moment that cicadas unleash a cry in unison.

Very quickly, it was very dark. Big clouds hid the moon and stars. The girls fell asleep. I waited for it to rain and could not fall asleep. Suddenly I saw, at the end of the path, a light flashing intermittently—another command to leave in the middle of the night, I thought, and I closed my eyes tightly, hoping to fall so soundly asleep that everyone would leave without me.

That's when my ear caught a familiar voice. I listened attentively. Yes! It was Sikoeun. I had heard one day that Sikoeun was seen near Boeng Béng.

His exit from Phnom Penh had been a kind of epic. He had gone to the radio station, as agreed, but had not found the army unit that was supposed to protect him. Respectful of discipline, he had waited quietly in the van.

Troops arrived, but they were Vietnamese. Sikoeun, his briefcase full of documents, along with his companions, took refuge in an office, waiting for the arrival of either a higher leader or the promised escort.

When the Vietnamese took over the building—which they did first thing, given its strategic location—Sikoeun and his group felt trapped. They played cat and mouse through the halls, moving from office to office and floor to floor, and were finally able to escape through a half-open door.

The crisis over, they waited to attempt an escape, having made up their minds that they would rather die than surrender.

During the night, they sent up a flare. There was no response. So they made their way through the brush and banana trees, scaled a wall, and ran to the nearby Tuol

Kok marsh. Unfortunately, they had left without being able to hide the documents left on the desks.

Plunging into the marsh, they walked and swam most of the night. At dawn they were in Prek Phneou, the north end of the town. There, they decided to separate into two groups: Sikoeun kept with him the heads of the English and Chinese sections, Ti and San (Soth's mother), while Phon left with the others.

Sikoeun and his companions took a route along the Battambang railroad tracks. They walked a long time without seeing anyone, when suddenly they spotted armed men coming toward them. They ran for shelter and jumped in a nearby pond. Large water lily leaves offered protection, however uncertain. Guns crackled. San called Sikoeun to her aid, for she had no more strength. But when the firing stopped, Sikoeun couldn't see Ti or San. He left alone and met In Sokan by chance in Pursat, as well as the other half of the group, which was still intact. From there, a liaison agent led them to Samlaut, where they joined the top leaders.

Sikoeun told me very proudly, that during the course of a meeting, Pol Pot had raised the issue of my evacuation, away from the hazards of war. "Only I told him I prefer that you stay."

The New Year arrived, as did the April 17 anniversary. Western journalists, led by a Thai peasant crying, "Friendship! Friendship!" came to photograph our encampment. The women, who made up the bulk of the group, took pains to show that morale was high. We had nothing to eat, but on the day agreed on for the celebration, two of our groups indulged in the privilege of sacrificing a cow, which meant much more meat than we could consume.

Béng was two months old. When his sisters talked to

him, he responded by watching them or by moving his little arms. He had a graceful, tender expression. But his father, always attentive to his image as a militant devoted to the party, pretended to ignore him. He spent his time moving from group to group to "take the pulse" of the people and talk to them. With his three pens in his shirt pocket, he didn't lack authority! He continued to criticize me publicly, reproaching me for living at the expense of the collective. On the day the cooks brought me an extra ration of meat, Sikoeun took it back to them.

During the night of April 17, a particularly violent storm broke out. The radio died. We quickly assembled our effects and several embers, to protect them from the rain.

The deluge was brief, however, and we prepared to go back to our rudely interrupted night. Suddenly a liaison agent cried, "We have to go."

"Not now," I protested. Sikoeun put on his backpack and took his position, waiting for others to follow. We didn't hear a sound. On such a night, during a storm, it was inconceivable that an enemy, even a commando, would come and dislodge us from this forsaken place. No one agreed to break camp.

We did have to leave the next day, however. We swallowed a flavorless beef soup, and, after throwing away or burying huge chunks of fresh meat (which we would later desperately wish we had), took to the road.

For the first time, we crossed the border into Thailand, while the radio blared patriotic and joyous songs recorded six months earlier. Four years to the day after having taken it, we had to flee Cambodia.

Four years earlier, the cannons had been silenced. A song of hope and peace had raised itself from the united hearts of the people. . . . And since then, we had lived in fear. We had seen disappearances multiply. There had been no tomorrows that sang and we now had the conviction that there never would be.

As I did at every departure, I asked myself, Why flee? and, How do I escape this situation? I was neither free nor my own master. I had to follow.

I wrapped the baby snugly in the *krâmar*, placed the bundles on my daughter's backs, and grabbed my bag. Béng wasn't heavy, but after a few steps, my legs weakened and I stumbled on a root. People helped me back to my feet and I wobbled on.

We crossed the stream that marked the border, then crossed a field and hoisted ourselves onto an embankment where the road passed.

A car full of young women in bright colors drove by, soon followed by another car packed with big, strong men dressed in shorts, who sang while someone banged a drum.

Being back in the civilized world was a shock. I had lived for so long with thin people dressed in black!

The Thai army arrived promptly to staunch the flood of refugees. It ordered combatants to leave their weapons and showed us the road to take to a coconut grove. The path was muddy and steep. Dizziness gripped me and I took a step backward. I couldn't make myself jump forward the way the soldiers wanted; my legs were simply too feeble, and besides, I had the baby in my arms. So there was nothing I could do but sit down and let myself slide down the hill, as if on a toboggan. It reminded me of a heroic episode in Mao's Long March, when the combatants let themselves slide down a snowy slope. They were lucky, I thought to myself, snow is clean!

We walked for a long time before reaching the coconut grove, and it was almost nightfall when we arrived. I gathered three dry palm fronds and lined them up under a tree to make a bed on the wet ground.

The children were already soundly asleep when Ra, from the Phnom Penh artistic ensemble, appeared, gesturing and shouting, "Lights! Lights! The Vietnamese are coming! Leave quickly!" Ra kept on spreading the panic as many people started running toward the road.

"If they are Vietnamese," I told him, "let them come and get us. I am going to sleep!"

The border post lights went out just before dawn.

We left the grove and headed south. "The Vietnamese are chasing us from the north, so we'll return by the south!" people said.

Path after path, field after field, we continued the march. Not knowing where we were going made it all the more exhausting. We finally reached a wide, sandy route that had become the theater for an indescribable procession. As far as the eye could see was a line of buffalo and cattle harnessed to miserable carts escorted by completely dispossessed poor people. Tens of thousands marched silently, staring ahead, in their dusty black clothes.

In the *krâmar*, Béng started to cry. He had not had any food in twenty-four hours. I tried to breast-feed him as we walked. He sucked at the teat a couple of times, then fell asleep.

Narén and Sokha, in turn, complained about thirst. They also had not had anything to drink since the day before. The sand burned the soles of our feet, the sun dried our throats. I didn't have enough breath to encourage them. I concentrated all of my energy on not falling. It was useless to stop. One had to wait for the decision to be made at the head of the line and then try to make it to the resting place in time to eat and drink something. No, we had to move ahead—move ahead under the midday sun, in the burning dust, tongues swollen, eyes burning, legs wobbling.

I spotted people from B1 on the roadside. I stopped, hoping to get some rice bouillon for the baby and the girls.

"We were waiting for you, Aunt Phâl," they said, coming to meet me and leading me away from the road.

I found Sikoeun holding a meeting. He got up and said, "The Vietnamese want B1 people. They have informants in the crowd. The watchword is 'look for a French woman!' That's easy, it's you!"

I wrapped my head in the *Krâmar* and we hurried on.

Villagers in colorful sarongs and wearing makeup stood in front of their houses and watched us pass. Compared to them, I felt like we were leaving a concentration camp or that we had returned from a trip in primitive times. When they saw my daughters, they exclaimed, *"Farang! Farang!"* ("Whites! Whites!") From village to village, the cry was repeated.

At the end of the afternoon, Thai army trucks intervened to organize the flood of refugees in a large, empty field divided by a stream. Everyone hurried to the water to bathe. The buffalo did the same. By the time the girls and I were able to make our way, we could draw only one little pan of water.

News about where we were going circulated. We would reenter Cambodia from the south, about 100 or 150 kilometers from our present position. It was guerrilla warfare, we were told, the long march to victory.

At night, B1 units grouped loosely away from the rest, clinging to the edge of a half-dried-up river. The next day, we took up the pathway again, amid the tinkling of cowbells, between cattle, buffalo, and carts, under the burning sun, in the dust, subject to the curious looks of villagers and the obscenities of Western journalists.

The route was long, very long for our exhausted bodies and hopeless hearts. Each minute lasted a decade. The sun never seemed to stop burning or putting mirages of trees in front of our reddened eyes. All along the teeming, scorching trails, there wasn't a bit of shade or a drop of water.

Sokha was the first to succumb to fatigue. She started to moan as she dragged her feet along. Her father decided to take care of the situation and hit her so hard that the crowd intervened. The child was so exhausted that she was reduced to a lump, and even the most violent blows would not put her back on her feet. Privately, she had chosen death.

I followed the road with Narén, advising her to walk in my shadow. The little angel was quiet, not voicing even one complaint. The burning heat brought us to the end of our strength, and our thirst provoked dizziness. But to stop was impossible. I begged Narén to make an effort, and then another effort. Soon I stopped talking altogether. I could no longer make myself understood and the little one could no longer hear.

Far off in the distance, we could see a dead tree. I pointed it out to her with my finger and told her we finally had a place to stop. To get there, she should count to a thousand. But at one thousand, the tree was still far off. It even seemed to get farther away as we approached. A sharp pain erupted in my back. Both the child and the bundle I was carrying on my back had slipped down to the end of my spinal column. It hurt so much that I wasn't able to shift the bundles myself. I tried to turn my head a little, but couldn't. I called out to my daughter, but, too tired to speak, she didn't answer. In one final effort, I yelled, "Quickly!"

We had to reach the dead tree quickly. Falling behind meant falling and never getting up. So we gathered the last of our energies to try to reach the tree under which an exhausted crowd waited to regain its strength.

Yan came to meet me, supporting me with his strong arm. I let the tears fall. (Tradition holds that above all, one should not cry—to cry was to yield.)

I gave myself a half-hour to rest, then another half-hour. Fatigue gave way to anxiety. Sokha and her father had not arrived. I questioned the people I knew who were passing: no one had seen them.

Another half-hour passed. Still nothing. I was tempted to go back and look for them, but I could not ask my exhausted daughter to do so. I also needed to think about going faster so that I might get to the front and find some food for Béng.

Yan left. I decided to follow her—I could count on her. Back on the road, we were told that there was a watering hole five kilometers ahead. I found Sokha and Sikoeun there.

We carried on.

At the end of the afternoon, the flood of refugees once again left the road for an empty field.

This field, like the last one, was filthy. Cattle, buffalo, and people had left excrement everywhere. We walked into the middle of it while trying to avoid it. People slept and ate in the midst of this filth. One watering hole was all there was for everyone. It was no longer hell, it was the pit of a latrine.

"Go left, after the second kapok tree, then right," I was told in order to find the place reserved for our unit. This time we skirted under some trees. The watering hole supplied just enough to make some rice bouillon. Since the day of the storm, I had not been able to wash, and I was covered with mud. Along the way, the young combatants managed to refresh themselves and change wherever water was available. I admired the way they took this vagrant life as if it were just a distraction from the routine. They were completely natural.

The next day, we went just a short way before stopping in a forested area with a stream. We reveled in the water, scraping ourselves with round stones to remove the layers of filth and mud. Bathing was as comforting as a good meal. We used branches and leaves to make beds and got ready for a good sleep. Suddenly, gunfire broke out. We quickly put out the coals and gathered our things, holding our hands over the mouths of the children who woke up. Then we waited, holding our breath and scanning the dark night.

A few seconds later, news reached us like a fresh breeze: robbers had attacked the camp and taken cattle, buffalo, and a young girl. . . .

The meager reserves of rice were gone. All we had left to eat for the next day were some wild grasses, which are succulent in soup but have no nutritional value, and are hard to swallow in water without salt. When we had to leave again, I was terribly weak. My head was spinning, my legs refused to obey, and my knees trembled. But I gritted my teeth and, in a desperate effort, breathed hard: You have to go, hang on! Hang on!

I took a step, then two, three, ten, thirty, fifty—I was off again!

For another whole day, we walked with the endless procession, surrounded by the tinkling and ringing of the cattle, buffalo, and carts. Early that afternoon, the sky darkened and the weather became very muggy. A big storm was about to erupt. Deprived as we were, there was nothing we could do but keep moving and hope to reach shelter. When the cloud burst a few hundred meters ahead of us, it dumped sheets of rain. Phon grabbed a piece of plastic material to protect Béng and the things, and we waited for the downpour to pass.

Then we carried on until nightfall. At the stopping point, we stretched out on wet branches after a futile attempt to start a fire. And at daybreak, we started off again.

This stretch was supposed to be the last. The leaders, I

figured, were surely going to do something for the children and me. I knew that Sikoeun had declined a job for me, working at the rear of the line, under the pretext that the iron was not yet hot and that this was a unique opportunity to harden it. He wanted to make me a heroine of the long march.

I wanted no part of the role of heroine. Crossing rivers on slippery tree trunks with the baby in my arms, drawing water at the bottom of steep slopes, blowing on coals to rekindle the fire, cutting wood, preparing beds made of leaves, and finding food was the most that my physical state and my inexperience allowed me to accomplish.

"Two kilometers after an irrigation pipe lying on the side of the road, you'll abandon the path and go left on a footpath in the forest," we were told. All of B1 would assemble there beyond the clearing,

We sat under trees so that we wouldn't be spotted by planes. For the same reason, we forbade people to put clothes out to dry in the sun. Barely even settled in, the leaders started to develop projects: we would have sewing machines brought in and a rear-base camp for the army installed.

Sikoeun had already been contacted by a liaison agent about meeting the leaders. He didn't hide his joy. I begged him to take us; at stake was the life of his infant son and two little daughters. Sikoeun rebuffed each of my arguments.

The man I was facing had only one goal: to leave as quickly as possible to wherever his mission called him. His mission exalted him and he exalted in it. To make it more sublime, he was prepared to make any sacrifices, and the most precious sacrifices of all were one's children and wife.

At the end of the argument, I blurted, "If it's like that—" and I stopped myself, knowing that I had already said too much. I had decided to go to the first Thai village with a police or army station and ask for asylum to ensure the survival of my children.

Sikoeun wouldn't budge. He simply got up, put on his backpack, and left. I saw him exchange words with the person in charge. Five minutes later, a combatant was posted near me, under the pretext of watching the baby. I understood. I was under surveillance. My fate had been decided.

In the heart of the Thai forest, the wait began. Members of the group began the search for those people who had not been able to follow. They compared themselves to a Vietcong resistance in Cambodia during the American war. Seen from this point of view, the catastrophe could be portrayed with cosmetic words of dignity and strength. Since we had beaten the Americans, we were going to make short work of the Vietnamese! We would let them scatter and then eliminate them once and for all in one blow.

To pass time, people who had been at the Descartes High School in Phnom Penh got together and rehashed old memories. They saw themselves again in front of their cheeses, desserts, and ice cream: "For my part, I liked the blue!"

"That was not as good as a Camembert softened just perfectly!"

"Tatin tarts? I don't know those, but oh those crêpes flambés!"

"I am going to tell you about a first-rate little restaurant where they serve huge platters of seafood and big, juicy steaks! I can still taste them!"

"And the breakfasts with croissants, jam, and coffee!"

I followed these wanderings of the imagination with a detachment that surprised me. Having dreamed all these years of a simple chunk of bread, I didn't want anything—except to leave.

I was stretched out. I began to shiver. Fever took over. Malaria would not leave me.

After the crisis passed, I was still weak. They brought medicines and a can with two sardines: a luxury that I shared with the children over two meals.

The whole community, despite seeming solidarity, had become antagonistic, and it seemed I could do nothing without provoking criticism or warnings.

The water problem became acute. Everyone washed their clothes and cleaned themselves in the one tiny watering hole. It was nauseating. Waste, from all the cases of dysentery, doubled. To find clear water, one had to dig a hole and wait. It pearled, drop by drop. It took a long time, but it was clear water.

One afternoon, little Béng played with me for the first time. After pretending to be scared, he threw me an accomplice's glance, proudly tossed his head on its side and smiled, with those adorable dimples. I took the child in my arms and embraced him, then cried with joy.

A moment later, he had runny stools. What I had dreaded the most had happened. I felt the hand of death on us and was once more overtaken by malaria's violent shaking.

The next morning, orders were given to pack for our return to Cambodia. Because we were taking the situation back into our own hands and because we were unable, like the Vietnamese, to organize the resistance from a foreign country, we had to leave immediately.

This long and complicated journey was just like the others. We would go around the mountain and, after crossing the plain, arrive at Sala Krao, near Pailin, where people would receive us by slaughtering a pig—always the same old song. And of course, we left without provisions.

From the bottom of my heart, I still hoped and had confidence. At Sala Krao, I had heard, there was a first aid center. Children were treated there. I could take Béng there. His sweet, mischievous expression kept coming to mind.

My bodyguard—to use the term loosely—carried my bundle once I had tied it up. But when I needed the rice bouillon for the baby, she was far away, and by the time I found her, the bouillon had soured.

I couldn't say anything. My despair at being powerless took over again. I walked like an automaton, prey to fever. Several times I heard cascades of clean water and wanted to run to quench my thirst, then realized that they were fever-induced mirages.

Instead of going around the mountain, this time we climbed it. The slope was steep. We often had to get down on our hands and knees.

It was heart-rending to see two women who had given birth the day before climbing and crawling.

The moment we reached the top, a combatant, seemingly from out of nowhere, shouted that we had no right to pass: military secret! He wanted us to turn back. We sat down. He left to discuss it with his superiors and then came back and gave us the green light. Still, we had lost precious time.

We walked for a long time following the rocky, flooded riverbed, then spilled out onto a path. Triumphant, the scouts announced that we had reached Cambodian territory. Nothing was known about the origin and use of the track. The path was straight, wide, and in good condition. It appeared to have been recently cleared. I just concentrated on walking.

My head was spinning. Ri, my neighbor, told me that I had spun around twice before collapsing with the baby in my arms.

Ri sounded the alarm. Young women from Mân's group came over. They knew what to do. They put their bundles down and pulled out a hammock. Others went to cut a branch. Moments later, they had a stretcher. They placed it alongside my body and lifted me gently onto it.

Already I could imagine Sikoeun accusing me of sucking the blood and sweat from my compatriots, but I let myself be carried anyway.

They left me at the stopping place and positioned me as comfortably as possible. Laên, overflowing with maternal love, took care of Béng. Lay took care of the girls, cooked rice, and found us a bit of fish paste. For her part, Ri gave me an orchid, a gem the color of pink as hot as a drop of water at sunset.

I was comforted by this but still unable to swallow any food. It was decided to wait for a truck that was supposed to bring supplies and pick up those too sick and weak to travel. All day we saw empty trucks go by. In mid-afternoon, Lay went to look for a bucket of water so that I could wash myself.

Ironically, I was in the process of washing my face when Choeun came to ask if I intended to stay, as everyone else had left!

I saw that the promise of the truck was just another lie. I gathered my things. But the moment we were about to leave, Narén refused to get up and cried, making our hearts melt. The poor child was exhausted. Thi and Lay ran over and talked to her gently. The child consented to follow them.

It was supposedly just eight kilometers to the watering hole, which was very close to our destination. Lay and Laên came to ask how I was holding up and suggested putting me back on the stretcher. I declined. Carrying a sick person, even one as light as I was, required a lot of effort. The young women chosen to carry me were strong but had not eaten in two days.

I staggered a lot in the first hundred meters, but after a while I steadied myself with the help of a walking stick. The trail was very long. Looking behind me, I realized that despite a great deal of effort, I wasn't getting very far. Night fell and we still hadn't arrived. We were thirsty— so thirsty that Narén and Sokha begged me to let them drink some of the black water in the ruts made by trucks. At first I said no, but I ended up consenting.

In my *krâmar*, the baby neither cried nor moved. His diarrhea, after subsiding momentarily, recurred. When I heard him empty himself again, my strength left me. Obstinately, I clung to the idea that we would soon come to Sala Krao, where he would be treated and saved.

Then I collapsed again. The carriers took over and our marathon continued.

The trail opened at last onto a clearing bathed in moonlight. We stopped. I lifted the baby from the *krâmar*. Under the moon, his face was ghastly and rings of death circled his eyes. I pressed him hard against my chest while cursing the moon. I asked for the doctor, but no one had seen him. We should have prepared a little rice bouillon for the baby, but there wasn't a drop of water.

The infant sucked desperately at my breast but it gave only a clear liquid.

As for Narén and Sokha, no one knew where they were. Far behind, no doubt. But then very shortly they arrived in the clearing, the older child holding the younger one's hand. They clutched a little tin of balm which they rubbed on their tummies, naively trying to wipe out the germs from the muddy water they had drunk as well as the hunger that gripped them.

Narén stretched out beside me and asked me to tell her about my grandmother. I told Narén about her sweet, patient face with a halo of white hair around it, her affectionate and humble smile, her generous heart. . . . In recalling her, I felt she was close, even though my past seemed completely foreign to me.

We broke camp at dawn. By the end of the morning, we still had not reached our goal—and still not a single watering hole.

In crossing Aur Da, we encountered combatants from Phnom Penh, dressed in black, who told us that a cholera epidemic had claimed two of their comrades.

By chance, a jeep approached and the people stopped. Sala Krao was still ten kilometers away, they told us, but we could not continue on this trail because the town was now occupied by Vietnamese.

Instead, we were directed toward Kâmrieng, situated near the border, which used to be the army's headquarters. Cheam, a B1 elder and member of a national ethnic minority, had installed his communications network and command post there. Several defense installations protected the post, which lay adjacent to a stream running along the border.

Life at Kâmrieng could have been agreeable, but death camped there. Flies glued themselves to the baby's emaciated face; a flick of the hand was not enough to chase them away. There was no medicine, although some was expected from Thailand. To stop the child's torture, I put him in the hammock and covered him with my *krâmar*. With its black and white squares, it was unbearable to look at, as it resembled a sarcophagus.

Then came the report that Sikoeun was back, that he was eating a special meal at the headquarters (that's where leaders and their wives ate mushrooms, fish, and other items in abundance).

Sikoeun never asked about his family, nor was he concerned when told that his son was sick. He only boasted about having covered in one stretch the distance we had taken several days to navigate.

At the end of the afternoon, I called for the doctor: Béng had vomited. A new doctor, an older man, came. He gave me medicines and exact instructions.

Béng seemed better. His cheeks were pale, but he opened his big round eyes, now without rings, played with his tiny hands, and showed off his dimples. He was a sweetheart. We spent the whole night together, intimately, in happiness.

In the morning, I was happy to announce that he had spent a good evening. While washing him, though, I was alarmed to find him so thin, so light.

I went to wash the baby's dirty sleeping mat in the stream. The effort drained me and I went back inside to lie down. In his hammock, the baby moaned. I prepared his medicine and asked Narén to bring me the baby. I grew impatient when she acted as if she were unable to pick up her brother. She said she was having difficulty. Finally she brought out little Béng: he was stiff with his hands turned backward.

I called Sikoeun to come and help me. He was ten steps away but acted deaf. When he decided to come, people had already gathered around the baby. "There is no need to cry like that," he yelled. "He is dying."

I cried.

Two doctors arrived immediately and they tried giving

212

him a long-awaited injection of serum. The cardiac stimulant caused Béng to cry one more time. His cries became more spaced, then he gasped. We closed his eyelids and crossed his delicate little hands on his chest.

It was May 10, a little after noon.

I didn't want to look at Béng. His face was no longer that of the child whom I had carried and who had smiled at me.

In the depths of poverty, he had nothing but his silk clothes. They wrapped him in red and gold silk. He remained what he was: an angel from beyond.

Little Béng, you are for me the blue heavens. I look at the azure sky, I think of you, I know you are there.

· *Epilogue* ·

The days and weeks that followed our departure were another long march with death—by disease, gunfire, mines, and drowning—taking the lives of almost all the babies, then the older children, adolescents, young women, and adults.

The leaders, then installed in a house in Thailand surrounded by a big field and busily organizing the anti-Vietnamese resistance, summoned Sikoeun and a few other survivors from the Ministry of Foreign Affairs to carry out a diplomatic journey in Asia. During the stopover in Peking, Ieng Sary appointed Sikoeun to the honorific position of minister-counselor at the Cambodian embassy.

At the same time, cloaking his action in effusive compassion, Ieng Sary gave orders for the girls and me to be taken from a disease-ridden camp and welcomed in his new government base where we were supposed to be safe, and to restore our health before taking on a new mission. The Khmer Rouge language was thus the same: promise of a mission signified a trap. During the trip, the liaison agent abandoned us in an open field. We learned later from another liaison agent who rescued us, that the field was within range of the enemy's guns. Later, on two separate occasions, I caught a so-called doctor in the process of forcing a very thin Narén to take medicines meant to kill her off. Through an intermediary, Ieng Sary demanded that Narén and Sokha, at that time nine and seven and a half years old, be sent to the front to prove themselves as combatants. Ignoring my scruples concerning the harm that I risked bringing to Sikoeun, I made plans to escape. Outwitting the military's vigilant watch was not a simple matter, but it was necessary to move quickly.

Then, contrary to all expectations, the Khmer Rouge told me they would keep their word and would arrange to have me leave with the girls and a group of foreigners—a group visiting Phnom Penh prior to the Vietnamese invasion and forced to follow the exodus for months—on the next day's flight to Peking.

It was August 11, 1979.

At the Cambodian embassy, we could more or less take care of ourselves and, after begging for months, I arranged for the girls to go to school.

In Peking, our life, as far as the Chinese were concerned, was marvelous. All three of us have rich and intense memories of it.

On the other hand, in terms of the Khmer Rouge, life was "come what may!" Allotted work, as before, was not compensated. Food was parsimoniously distributed. One had to beg for clothes and medicine. Surveillance was around the clock. All that was said and not said, every fact and gesture continued to be compiled, analyzed, and interpreted. Deep inside, I wanted very much to be done with the Khmer Rouge. With every beat, my heart repeated: get away, get away . . .

As sometimes happens to people who want so much for something to happen, I experienced a phenomenon some call mediumistic and others call divine or prophetic—all the necessary signs to achieve my wish and, while I worried about the risks incurred, confidence that everything would work out.

Three months later, one year to the day after our arrival

216

in Peking, August 11, 1980, we left for the Khmer Rouge government base on the Khmer-Thai border. Shortly after our arrival, Sikoeun went on a mission to the United Nations. The children and I, as part of another diplomatic mission, were sent to Geneva fourteen weeks later. Still, I had to use all the tact I was capable of and all my reserves of determination, waiting five long weeks to touch French soil and return to my family. It was Christmas Eve. Oh, how symbolic!

My family welcomed us with open arms, without skimping on time, money, or effort. At every turn, they engulfed us with care and warm affection. My mother came out of retirement to ensure us of her support; my sister gave us all the things she could to allow us to live; and my brother gave us lodging in the countryside to guarantee our safety and to enable me to give birth, under the best conditions, to the child I was expecting and who I named Nicolas.

I also immediately asked for a divorce and gained custody of the children. Thus I regained and wrote under my maiden name. Sikoeun came several times to France to take away the children who, as he put it, should die on the battlefield against Vietnam.

During one of his visits which my family arranged far from my home, with a concern for honesty, I warned him that I was writing a book. I wanted to put him on guard against any possible repercussions, since I respect that which is divine in marriage, which divorce does not dissolve.

That is how he came to deliberately choose to stay with the Khmer Rouge. The reasons for his choice are many. On one hand, he was afraid to relearn; to live a normal life: all the difficulties I encountered in finding a modest job could only have discouraged him from taking this route. On the other hand, he undoubtedly still dreamed of sublimating himself through self-sacrifice for his country. He still writes once or twice a year, four or five lines, always the same, in which he says he carries on his fight.

In this summer of 1988 Narén is seventeen years old, Sokha will soon be sixteen, and Nicolas seven. Their school grades are very good. For my part, in addition to my role as head of a family and my work, I am taking courses to train for a new profession. We are all happy and in good health.

One source of our happiness is indeed the situation in Cambodia which we follow in its evolution toward that which we hold so deeply at heart: namely, peace. We are happy to see rising from the ashes a phoenix that will soon create, in a country favored by nature, a new political, social, and economic order and a new social being.

I have not forgotten, I do not want to forget, I am afraid of forgetting.

I hope my book merits attention especially for the spirit in which it is written. I wanted my experience to be known and, if I rejoice greatly in seeing it translated into English, it is not that I pity myself for my tragic fate nor that I look passively at a life with its procession of sufferings and acts of courage, hope, and despair. It is written in order that the greatest possible number of people search themselves, realize their potential, bad as well as good, build themselves psychologically and meditate on the meaning and symbolism of life, to go beyond good and evil, and to act and build together a humane world, a world without war and without hatred.